EastEnders

Real **Soap**

EastEnders

Real **Soap**

Karen Sinotok

generation

DEDICATED TO: SIAM & EASTENDERS FANS EVERYWHERE
ESPECIALLY ORLA AND CATH AT GEORGE TINGLE HOUSE

ACKNOWLEDGMENTS:

A special thanks to: Mike Wood, Eddie Schillace, Paul Sudbury,

Eve Cousins, Phil McNeill, Caroline Machin, Joe Crowe

PHOTOGRAPHIC ACKNOWLEDGMENTS:

All photographs courtesy of Rex

Real Soap: EastEnders was first published in Great Britain in 1999 by

Generation Publications ltd

11-12 Tottenham Mews

London W1P 9PJ

CIP data for this title is available from the British Library

ISBN 1 903009 04 9

Book and jacket Design Generation Studio

Reprographics by Media Print (UK) Ltd.

Printed and bound in Spain by Bookprint, S.L., Barcelona

WELCOME TO...

Ever been to Walford?

Course you 'ave!

LONDON BOROUGH OF WALFORD
ALBERT SQUARE
E 20

In the beginning,
BBC created women
– with ATTITUDE

Foreword

EVER SINCE THE OPENING CREDITS WITH THE LONG AND WINDING RIVER, AND THAT SOON-TO-BE-FAMILIAR THEME TUNE, *EASTENDERS* HAS TAKEN A MORBID PLEASURE IN DELVING INTO THE MURKY UNDERSIDE OF LONDON LIFE.

AFTER THE EARLY 1980S GLITZ AND GLAMOUR OF AMERICAN SHOWS SUCH AS *DALLAS* AND *DYNASTY*, THIS HOME-GROWN SOAP SHOWED THE BRUTAL REALITY OF URBAN LIVING – AND WHAT BETTER WAY TO KICK OFF THE SHOW THAN WITH A CORPSE?

STARTING AS IT MEANT TO GO ON, *EASTENDERS'* OPENING EPISODE IN 1985 FEATURED THE FIRST OF SO MANY STIFFS TO APPEAR IN ALBERT SQUARE, A CHARACTER WITH THE SHORTEST SCREEN LIFE OF ANY – REG 'BLINK AND YOU MISS ME' COX...

CRITICS CALLED THE SOAP DEPRESSING, BUT THE PUBLIC LOVED IT, AND SOON THE CLASSIC CHRISTMAS DAY EPISODES WERE AS MUCH OF A TRADITION AS THE QUEEN'S SPEECH (THOUGH WITH RATHER MORE GORE) AND OVERSHADOWING THE MIGHTY CORRIE IN THE RATINGS.

EASTENDERS' STRENGTH HAS ALWAYS BEEN ITS ABILITY TO BRING US BRILLIANTLY BELIEVABLE CHARACTERS. THE WARRING WATTS, SEX-CRAZED BITCH CINDY BEALE, CUTE BUT TROUBLED JOE WICKS, CHAIN-SMOKING DOT, THE HARD-NUT MITCHELL BRUVVERS, EVIL STEVE OWEN, TRAGIC TIFFANY, WHINGING BIANCA...

THE SERIES' CREATORS WANTED REALISM, AND, BY CASTING GENUINE EAST END ACTORS WITH COCKNEY ACCENTS YOU COULD CUT GLASS WITH, THEY SOMETIMES GOT MORE THAN THEY BARGAINED FOR. WITH THEIR RIOTOUS PERSONAL LIVES, THERE WERE TIMES WHEN THE OFFSCREEN RUCKS AND ROWS OF THE CAST WERE MORE OVER-THE-TOP THAN ANYTHING THE SCRIPTWRITERS COULD EVER HAVE DREAMED UP.

SUICIDE, MURDER, GANGSTERS, DRINK AND DRUGS BINGES, SEX SCANDALS... THE REAL-LIFE STORIES OF THE REAL *EASTENDERS* ARE JUST AS OUTRAGEOUS AS ANYTHING YOU'LL EVER SEE ON THE TELLY...

Mark won the silly hat award

THE FOWLERS

WENDY RICHARD (AKA PAULINE FOWLER)

Pauline's a woman for whom family is everything. Unfortunate then, that there are so few Fowlers left with whom she can share a pot of Tetley's finest.

Most of her relatives are either dead or overseas, leaving Pauline with a cupboard full of unused teabags and an even more miserable expression than usual.

But, though Pauline's had more than her fair share of knocks, she won't let life get her down. With a gymslip mum for a daughter and an HIV positive son, this East End battler always muddles through somehow. But the death of her beloved husband Arthur was the cruellest blow of all...

The opening credits rolled and the nation drew a collective gasp of horror when Wendy Richard appeared as Pauline Fowler in the first *EastEnders*. Grown men wept as they recalled their teenage crushes on the foxy, flirty Miss Brahms in *Are You Being Served?* Could this middle-aged woman with the straggly hair and droopy cardie have been their '70s pin-up? What was she doing in such a depressing kitchen, married to that old man?

Like Babs Windsor before her, Wendy was a very British showbiz icon. Some thought she was brave to shed her sexy sitcom image, but the actress didn't mind at all, saying she was sick of glamour and wanted to play her age.

Still, her looks never harmed her career. After drama school she cornered the market in mini-skirted dolly birds, appearing in nudge-nudge, wink-wink British comedies *On The Buses*, *Please Sir*, and, of course, as the buxom Miss Brahms, always ready to swap a *double entendre* about Mrs Slocombe's pussy in *Are You Being Served?*

But offscreen Wendy's private life was touched by tragedy. Her parents ran a pub and, when she was just 11, her father committed suicide by gassing himself. Wendy was the one who found him. Then, just as her acting career was really taking off, her mum died of cancer.

The leggy blonde wasn't so lucky in love either. Her first marriage lasted all of five months, while her second husband beat her up. It was third time unlucky when she wed Irish carpet fitter Paul Glorney.

Though she claimed in 1993 that the marriage couldn't be happier, they broke up a year later. Divorced after he admitted adultery, he told the press her drinking broke up the marriage.

It's all a far cry from her one-man woman screen character. Pauline had never had eyes for anyone but her Arfur, and so was shattered to discover he'd been having an affair. One of the most unlikely candidates for sex romps, she was stunned (as were we all) at the idea of stay-at-home Arfur doing the bedroom cha-cha with Lizzie Powers.

Her marriage to Arfur stretched her loyalties and tea-making abilities to the limit. The kettle was never off the boil as she lived through his affair, nervous breakdown (and what a cheerful Christmas Day show that was for viewers in 1986), and imprisonment for a crime he didn't commit. Just when it seemed like they were coming through the worst, he went and dropped dead on his allotment. Typical man, eh?

If glamour was in short supply at 45, Albert Square, there was no shortage of drama. In fact, after 14 years ruling the roost, Pauline Fowler is such a

Gossip

WENDY RICHARD (AKA PAULINE FOWLER)

THE closest Wendy got in *EastEnders* to her sex symbol days of old was when Pauline won a glamorous granny competition in 1986.

IT'S not been all doom and gloom for Pauline. She once let her hair down and did a can-can at a Christmas party in the Queen Vic.

WENDY had a few nervous moments when it was feared she was being stalked by an obsessed fan. She was given a police guard for a while.

SHE adores her Cairn terrier, Shirley.

WENDY is a veggie.

WENDY earned £15 as the cockney girl's voice on Mike Sarne's hit record 'Come Outside', in 1962.

national institution it's hard to remember a time when she wasn't having her say about the latest ruckus over a hot wash at the launderette.

But it's Pauline's nasty habit of losing members of her family which marks her as someone you wouldn't want to be related to.

First she buried her mum, the sanctimonious old battleaxe Lou Beale, and then her twin brother Pete died in a car crash in December 1993 (yet another upbeat Christmas episode).

Even the living Fowlers are nowhere to be seen. Pauline's daughter Michelle disappeared off to Florida with Pauline's grand-daughter Vicki, while her elusive brother Kenny is in New Zealand.

That leaves just young, unplanned Martin, the result of a surprise middle-aged pregnancy, who's turned into a bit of a thieving wrong 'un, and her eldest, Mark – just don't mention the fact that his appearance changed overnight.

In real life Wendy never had kids, but her close circle of friends rallied round when the actress recently had a terrifying brush with cancer.

She discovered a lump in her breast, and was diagnosed as having breast cancer on Valentine's Day. Doctors removed a lump the size of a Cadbury's Creme Egg and, after radio-therapy, Wendy is all clear of the disease.

Wendy blames her cancer on stress, and has vowed to take life a bit easier. She's even found love again, with a man 16 years her junior, painter and decorator John Burns.

The girl's done all right out of her time in the Square and now lives in a posh four-storey house in London's West End and says fans can look forward to seeing Pauline's careworn face for years to come. 'I enjoy playing her too much to leave.'

BILL TREACHER (AKA ARTHUR FOWLER)

Poor Arthur. He started life in Albert Square as the loyal loving husband of Pauline, a devoted family man as straight as they come. All he wanted was an easy life, but by the time he popped his clogs 11 years later he'd turned into a cheating gigolo, suffered a mental breakdown and been locked up in prison twice.

The root of Arthur's personality change came when he stole the Christmas Club money to pay for daughter Michelle's non-event of a wedding. Banged up for a month, he was never the same again.

Soon, he was one of the least convincing adulterers ever seen on screen, carrying on an affair with the alluring Mrs Hewitt.

Kicked out by his outraged missus, Arfur's life went downhill fast, and he was heartbroken when accused of swindling £20,000 of council cash and thrown in jail. Even worse, evil Willy Roper – who had stolen the money – was making moves on Pauline.

The couple eventually patched things up, but Arf was a broken man and, in 1996, collapsed at his allotment and died in hospital.

By then, actor Bill Treacher had had enough and was delighted to quit the soap. 'When Arthur had a nervous breakdown, I felt I was going through it with him,' he confessed. 'I had to break out of that bloody bubble. It got to the point where my heart sank when I went through the studio gates.'

Arfur - the biggest turnip on the allotment

Lofty proving the theory that ignorance is truly bliss

SUSAN TULLY (AKA MICHELLE FOWLER)

Growing up on screen is never easy, but Susan Tully went through the mill as Michelle Fowler.

No stranger to telly, Susan starred in *Grange Hill* before *EastEnders*, but once out of her school uniform she was at the mercy of the soap writers.

And they really had it in for her. She was doomed to spend hours drinking tea in the kitchen with her mum Pauline and granny Lou Beale, listening to them bang on about the comings and goings in the Square.

An old head (with a dodgy perm) on young shoulders, poor 'Chelle ended up getting pregnant after a sordid one-nighter on the beer-sodden floor of the Queen Vic with her best mate's dad.

Being a single mum made 'Chelle even more of a downer than before, but the fact that she was a right misery guts didn't stop lovable simpleton Lofty falling in love, giving her a moment of TV glory when she jilted him at the altar in a 'will she, won't she?' cliff-hanger.

Michelle proved her fertility and unusual interpretation of the concept of friendship once again by shagging Shaz's husband Grant. (That's Grant as in the thug she'd always loathed with a passion.)

It was all very Freudian, and is probably, even now,

giving the shrinks in America, where she lives with Vicki (named after the pub she was conceived in – how tasteful) and Grant's baby, a run for their money.

In between dropping sprogs, 'Chelle went out with young black single father Clyde, and had an affair with her college tutor Geoff Barnes. She thought about moving up North to be with him but, as he was older than her dad and not related to Sharon in any way, decided against it.

In real life, Susan has led a remarkably normal life and has no time for any showbiz attitude. 'My family and friends keep me sane,' she says. 'My family still lives on the same council estate where I grew up, and I have given strict instructions to my nearest and dearest to slap me down severely if I'm not behaving.'

Since leaving *EastEnders*, Michelle has moved to the other side of the camera and become a director – even directing six episodes of the show.

Bald patrol makes first sighting of Dirty Den

Gossip

SUSAN TULLY (AKA MICHELLE FOWLER)

INMATES at Dartmoor prison rioted when bad weather meant they lost BBC reception on their telly for 'Chelle's wedding that never was. One soap-rager convict yelled: '*EastEnders* is our favourite show and we all wanted to see if Lofty finally made it with Michelle.'

TODD CARTY (AKA MARK FOWLER)

As you'd expect from an Albert Square lifer, Mark Fowler has had more than his fair share of trouble, but actor Todd Carty's life couldn't be more different.

Already a familiar face to schoolkids everywhere as Tucker Jenkins in Grange Hill, and his own spin-off show, Tucker's Luck, Todd is pretty well-adjusted after spending his life in the public eye.

When he takes off his leather jacket and money belt (hardly bulging as his fruit'n'veg stall on Bridge Street only ever shifts the occasional apple), he reverts back to being Mr Average, going home to long-time girlfriend Dina and young son James.

'Being a dad is the best thing that's happened to me,' he says, rather rubbing salt in the wound of poor old Mark, whose HIV status put a dampener on his chances in that department.

Still, it did mean we've seen the last of his depressing Jock missus, Ruth (last seen legging it north of the border, carrying Conor's baby), so not altogether a bad thing. All the same, it's not much of a life for a young lad living with HIV and his mum, with only a bottle of Becks for entertainment of an evening. The good news is he looks the picture of health, though he's porking out so much he looks scarily like Barry.

Felling down, feeling depressed? Cheer up it could be worse - you could be Mark Fowler

Now, now Gillian stop slipping out of character...

GILLIAN TAYLFORTH
(AKA KATHY MITCHELL)

Gossip

GILLIAN TAYLFORTH
(AKA KATHY MITCHELL)

GILLIAN used to work in the BBC photo department.

GILLIAN first auditioned to play Sue Osman, Ali's wife. The part eventually went to ex-heroin addict Sandy Ratcliff.

HER mum wasn't too impressed when Gillian got the part. 'She thought I was going to tell her I'd got engaged.'

GILLIAN was gutted when Kathy's battered leather jacket was stolen off the set. 'Why couldn't they have taken that rotten blue woollen bobble hat instead?' she asked.

GILLIAN is close to screen son Adam Woodyatt. 'When he told me he was going to be a dad I was thrilled. It was as if my own son was telling me.'

SHE was romantically linked to co-star Nick Berry (her stepson in *EastEnders*) in real life.

Come back, Kaff! She might have been a weary 47-year-old divorcee, but when Kathy Mitchell packed her bags and headed off to start a new life in South Africa, half of the sperm-producing males in the Square were queuing up to beg her to stay. Even the vicar wasn't immune to her aging charms. But, as a woman for whom the phrase 'unlucky in love' might have been invented, it looked like she'd finally learned her lesson and she slipped away with barely a backward glance.

She coped with rape (twice), blackmail, a nervous breakdown and a violent drunken husband, before realising that, when your only comfort comes in the shape of depressing son Ian, it's time to get out.

She lived a hell of a life onscreen, and actress Gillian Taylforth's offscreen antics have been equally dramatic. Working as a secretary for a travel agency when she joined the cast as a fresh-faced 28-year-old,

she promised *EastEnders* bosses she'd have a few late nights to make sure she looked old enough to be Ian's mum. Sure enough, after a few gruelling years on the Square, she looked knackered enough to

'Don't worry Gillian, I think I've done a sponsorship deal with Range Rover'

court over a report that she and Knights had had a roadside sex session.

She denied she had been giving Geoff oral sex in their car claiming she had undone his trousers to ease the pain of pancreatitis. She was not going down on him, she declared, merely massaging his stomach.

Taylforth told the High Court that she felt 'unclean and ashamed' after reading the 1992 front page story. When accused of being a drama queen who was re-enacting the aftermath of her rape scene in EastEnders, Kathy gripped the rail of the witness box and replied: 'No, that was Kathy Beale. I'm Gillian Taylforth.'

Unfortunately for Gill, her attempts to portray herself as the last of the Walford virgins backfired

play Ian's granny.

But it was her out-of-control personal life which really etched the worry lines on to poor Gill's face.

One of four daughters from a close-knit North London family, her printer dad had strong moral values. 'We used to think he was too strict but we've all grown up to be decent people with the

discipline that was instilled in us,' she says.

Then, a few years into the soap, Gillian met volatile Geoff Knights, a millionaire businessman, and soon their public rucks made big news. He had convictions for burglary and assault and is alleged to have dragged her out of bed once so savagely that she fell and fractured her nose.

They had a baby daughter, Jessica, but then in 1994 came the libel case that nearly destroyed them, when Gillian took *The Sun* to

Classic Kathy quote

'I'VE HAD MORE FRESH STARTS THAN LINFORD CHRISTIE'

when the defence showed a video of her sucking playfully on a German sausage at a wild party.

The case crumbled and, landed with a legal bill of £250,000, the couple were forced to sell their homes. Even Knights' beloved Ferrari had to go, when he was declared bankrupt

'It's been soul-destroying for him,' said Gillian.

Even after the court case, Gill's troubles were far from over. A year later she was arrested for drink-driving after crashing her BMW with daughter Jessica in the back after a boozy cast party.

The actress admitted that at one point she thought of suicide.

'Whichever way I turned there were problems, or another smutty joke. I never imagined I'd get in such a state, but then I went upstairs, saw Jessie lying in bed and thought, "What's the matter, you imbecile?"'

In fact, it was *EastEnders* which kept

her sane, saying the show was a rock. 'Whenever something terrible has happened I've gone back into work and the people there have supported me.'

Onscreen, as a study in misery, you wouldn't have to look much further than Kathy's so-called life. Been there, done that, got the T-shirt – Kathy was a woman who took everything that the scriptwriters could throw at her.

From an uneventful start as loyal wife of fruit'n'veg king Pete 'The Prat' Dean, it seemed the most she had to worry about was having such a depressing son as Ian.

But, bit by bit, the horrible truth was revealed. She'd been raped at 14, and given her child up for adoption, only to have long-lost daughter Donna turn up a loony drug addict who eventually died from an overdose.

Kathy coped with being blackmailed by evil Nick Cotton and yet another rape, this time by posh but poisonous

Former EastEnders star is banned for drink-driving

FORMER EastEnders star Letitia Dean told magistrates she had 'no excuses' after admitting drink-driving yesterday.

Dean, 28, who played pub landlady Sharon Mitchell in the soap, was more than twice over the limit when she was stopped after clipping a kerb in her Mazda sports

car. Tower Bridge magistrates fined her £750 and imposed a two-and-a-half year ban. Looking pale and drawn and dressed in black, she told them: 'I am just very, very sorry.'

Magistrate David Cooper warned Dean, of Westminster: 'If you drive while you are disqualified, you will certainly go to prison.'

Dean: 'So sorry'

You'd have a drink problem too if you were married to Grant...

Pete's happy as long as he doesn't have to say ripe or raspberries

Gillian had no shortage of takers for a lift home in her car

James Wilmott-Brown. Not surprisingly, the gal had a nervous breakdown and her marriage to Pete collapsed.

She succumbed to the inarticulate charm of Phil, though the writing was soon on the wall, with her engagement party rather spoilt by the revelation that her hubby-to-be had been sleeping with his brother's wife.

But, hey, everyone's human and Kaff showed her usual forgiving nature and bad judgment by eventually marrying Phil and having baby Ben.

Somehow, she escaped dying in childbirth, but there was still trauma to come when Ben was rushed to hospital with meningitis. Meanwhile, Phil reacted to the joys of parenthood in true Mitchell style – by becoming a violent and abusive drunk. Our '90s New Man even started an affair with Lorna, a woman he met at Alcoholics Anonymous.

If that wasn't enough, there was the small matter of Cindy trying to bump off Ian. To cheer herself up, Kaff snogged Grant, then bedded vicar Alex, before deciding it was time to head for South Africa with brother Ted for a well-earned rest. For once, Kaff had learned her lesson – that men were her downfall.

As one observer put it: 'A woman for whom the light at the end of the tunnel is usually blue, flashing and accompanied by policemen with grave news,' the nation mourned as she arrived at the airport with her luggage in April 1998.

For Kathy was a peculiarly British icon. Exuding sex appeal as she furiously buttered endless loaves of sliced white bread in her caff, she's sadly missed.

But all is not lost. Gillian quit the soap to spend more time with her family, but though she loves being a full-time mum, she says she may come back.

Even she and Knights seem to have reached a truce. They're now engaged and, after two tragic miscarriages, have a new baby son, Harrison, born in March 1999, when Gillian was 43. They live in a bungalow in Hertfordshire and plan to marry in 2000.

Says Gill of their relationship: 'I love a good old ruck to clear the air, but we've been portrayed as always throwing pans at each other and that isn't true.

'Me and Geoff have stuck through problems that would've broken up a weaker relationship. We have grown up a bit and become a lot closer. Geoff has changed an awful lot. He's very soft-hearted.'

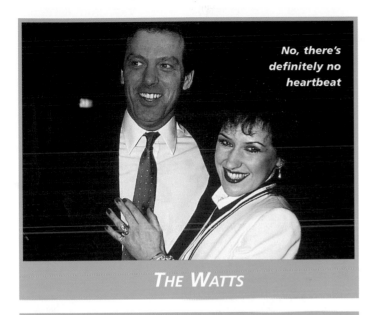

No, there's definitely no heartbeat

THE WATTS

ANITA DOBSON (AKA ANGIE WATTS)

Everything all right darlin'? Few of the punters in the Queen Vic had any idea of the ructions that were going on upstairs when the warring Watts were running the place. Her marriage was falling apart, but Angie hid her misery behind a painted smile.

The first, and some say finest, landlady of the Vic, Angie had her fair share of worries. And, faced with a husband who was more interested in walking the dog or sleeping with teenagers than showing her any affection, Angie took comfort in the bottle. A woman has needs, and hers weren't being met.

The Angie and Den show lurched from one vicious slanging match to another for three riveting years, as they slowly destroyed one another.

So depressingly accurate was the warring state of their marriage, that in 1986, when desperate Angie tried to top herself after Den had left her for his posh totty Jan Hammond, by washing down a bottle of sleeping pills with gin, in a worrying tale of life imitating art, the number of real East Enders treated for overdoses tripled that week.

There were no depths to which Angie wouldn't stoop to keep her man. When Den wanted a divorce, she even claimed she was dying.

A real East Ender, Anita Dobson was born in Stepney, and says that her screen family felt natural straight away.

'It all just clicked. Letitia Dean walked up to me and said, "Would you like a cup of tea, Mum?" I melted and got misty-eyed because there I was, 36 years old with no kids, and this adorable little blonde fluffball had suddenly been thrust into my arms and was calling me "Mum". It was great.'

She and Leslie Grantham didn't socialise offset though.

'We always went our separate ways after work. It made sense because Den and Angie's on-screen relationship was so extraordinary and intense.' Anita was nothing like her neurotic G&T swilling role,

Gossip

ANITA DOBSON (AKA ANGIE WATTS)

ANITA played a woman haunted by the spirit of her dead husband in a BBC play *I'll Be Watching You* – now there's a scary thought.

IN the book *Blood Ties: The Life and Loves of Grant Mitchell*, by Kate Lock, it's revealed that Angie lives in a kitsch mansion in Florida with her new husband who made a fortune in packaging.

DEN, Angie and Sharon were originally called Jack, Pearl and Tracey Watts.

30 million people watched the classic moment when Den handed Angie their divorce papers as a surprise present in Christmas 1986.

but blame her for Angie's tacky clobber, because she was the one who committed style suicide when she went shopping for her onscreen wardrobe.

She didn't have quite the same affection as the rest of the country for the Watts.

'Den and Angie were quite a sad couple. She pines for a guy who flaunts his mistress about! And, when *EastEnders* began, they hadn't slept with each other for ten years.'

Offscreen, unmarried Anita kept the tabloids happy by dating co-star Tom (Lofty) Watts, then having a long-term love affair with fellow poodle-perm Brian May from Queen. Their matching big hair could often be seen at various celeb dos, but her acting career never quite scaled those heady '80s heights again.

Her comeback show after quitting *EastEnders* was a hairdressing sitcom, *Split Ends*, which had the plug pulled on it after just one series. Then there was the West End stage flop *Budgie*, with Adam Faith, followed by another musical, *Eurovision*, which lasted just five days.

Since then, Anita has popped up on *Red Dwarf*, *The Bill* and *Rab C Nesbitt* and rules out returning to the show which made her a household name.

'I wouldn't hold out too much hope. Once somebody leaves, they usually don't come back. It's on to other things, away from the crazy ride of being on that show.'

She still retains affection for her alter ego Angie, though.

'I have a fantasy that she's made good in Florida. She's swathed head to foot in furs and has just had her first of many face-lifts. She's remarried – he's more than a bit younger than her...'

IT'S A FACT!

THE NAME WALFORD COMES FROM A MIXTURE OF WALTHAMSTOW AND STRATFORD

Smug or wot?

LESLIE GRANTHAM (AKA DEN WATTS)

A convicted murderer as the lead character in the new BBC soap? The press had a field day when it was revealed that Leslie Grantham had spent 11 years behind bars after he murdered a taxi driver as a young squaddie in Germany. He shot the man dead during an attempted robbery.

But Grantham was a reformed character, and credited prison with getting him into the acting game. He got involved in amateur dramatics while he was banged up, and successfully applied to drama school from jail.

Brought up on a council estate in South London, he sums himself up: 'Some people say I'm a nice guy, some say I'm a pile of poo. Somewhere in the middle is about right. I'm a nice pile of poo.' But it was as the sexy 'bit of rough' that was Grantham's finest hour. Everyone thought Dirty Den would meet a nasty end courtesy of a knife-wielding Angie after one G&T too many. But it was his dalliance with the criminal element of East London, the mysterious 'Firm' which proved to be the death of him. On the run from The Firm, he was shot by a mystery man holding a bunch of daffs, and his decomposed body was found in the canal a year later, thus putting an end to any lingering hope that he might be back.

Professionally, Grantham's done all right since quitting the soap. He starred in the hit gangster series *Paradise Club*, but his second, *99-1*, flopped. He wrote, produced and starred in sci fi drama *The Uninvited*, and starred as Colonel Mustard in telly whodunnit *Cluedo* (surely his finest acting hour). And he's got no regrets.

'I have a great lifestyle and I never stop working. I'm a very lucky guy.' A private man, devoted to his family, he says his wife, actress Jane Laurie, and his children are his greatest achievement. 'I'm most proud of having kids and getting married.'

Gossip

LESLIE GRANTHAM (AKA DEN WATTS)

LESLIE Grantham originally auditioned for part of Pete Beale.

HE used to work in an Italian clothes shop in Chelsea, and flogged frocks to Princess Di when she was plain Diana Spencer. She recognised him when she visited the *EastEnders* set.

HE even went back into the jail – Leyhill Open prison – where he was once a prisoner, to open a Picasso exhibition.

TALKING SHOP
Brothers in arms

Martin Kemp kept well out of it when three members of Spandau Ballet took his brother Gary to court. Singer Tony Hadley, drummer John Keeble and sax player Steve Norman sued for a share of the fortune songwriter Gary Kemp earned from a string of hits. But in June 1999, Gary won his High Court battle, leaving the 'devastated' trio with a legal bill of £200,000. No consolation then that the judge said he had enjoyed Spandau's music so much that he had kept the CD.

Steve McFadden - a lager than life character

150,000 other pubs in London and they choose to drink here!

TALKING SHOP

Don't give up the day job

EASTENDERS MAKING MUSIC

There have always been a lot of pop wannabes in Albert Square. Some fared better than others

PETER DEAN (Pete Beale): 'Can't Get A Ticket for The World Cup' – Chas'n'Dave-style singalong floperoonee (1986, reached No 121).

ANITA DOBSON (Angie Watts): The nauseating 'Anyone Can Fall In Love', sung to the *EastEnders* theme, got to No 4 in 1986. The follow-up, 'Talking of Love' stiffed at No 43.

TOM WATT (Lofty): His cover of the Bob Dylan classic 'Subterranean Homesick Blues' failed to impress the record-buying public. It reached a dismal No 134 in 1986.

LETITIA DEAN AND PAUL MEDFORD (Sharon Watts and Kelvin Carpenter): This unlikely duo's inane pop ditty, 'Something Outta Nothing', somehow made it to No 12 in 1986.

NICK BERRY (Simon Wicks): Wimpsome ballad 'Every Loser Wins' reached No 1 in 1986. The former Queen Vic barman only managed to get to No 42 with his follow-up, 'Long Live Love'.

SOPHIE LAWRENCE (Diane Butcher): Dreadful remake of 'Love's Unkind' reached No 21 in 1991. Even Sophie said: 'I hate that song.'

SEAN MAGUIRE (Aiden Brosnan): Reached No 14 with his first release 'Someone to Love' in summer 1994.

MICHELLE GAYLE (Hattie Tavernier): She quit the series after five years and was so serious about her music she sent demos out anonymously. Sexy and with more cred than other soap singers, she had a hit with the groovesome 'Sweetness' in 1994, married Sheffield Wednesday footballer Mark Bright in Las Vegas and got starring role in big budget musical *Beauty and the Beast* in London's Dominion Theatre.

BARBARA WINDSOR (Peggy Butcher): An album of pop standards in 1998 called 'You've Got A Friend'.

MARTINE McCUTCHEON (Tiffany Mitchell): No 1 with power ballad 'Perfect Moment'.

No believe me. You don't want me to switch it on

Pushing up the daisies

A recent survey showed that British soap opera characters are three times more likely to die violently than your average citizen, so it's a good idea to make sure your life insurance is up to date if you're planning a move to Albert Square.

In what's got to be one of the most dangerous places in the country to live (apart from Brookside Close), no fewer than 16 characters have met messy ends there in the past 14 years.

Now, we all know that London's East End isn't immune to the odd spot of argy-bargy, but this'd put the Kray twins' reign of terror to shame.

Surely it's time for a road safety talk at the very least...

Facts

THE brutal murder of Saskia Duncan shouldn't have been shown before nine o'clock. TV watchdog Broadcasting Standards Agency said the episode was far too graphic and disturbing for children. 'The explicitness of the violence and the macabre disposal of the body went beyond acceptable boundaries,' they blasted.

ACTOR Chris Hancock, who played Charlie Cotton, was philosophical about meeting his brutal end. 'I enjoyed the part, but that's showbiz...'

EVEN the dogs aren't safe. Animal lovers still shed a tear over canine fatalities Willie (Ethel's pug who snuffed it from old age) and Roly (Den's poodle, killed by a car). Wellard should be careful who he accepts a Bonio from then.

Sorry, but you're brown bread...

REG COX	(murder)
DEN WATTS	(shot)
EDDIE ROYLE	(stabbed, Nick Cotton charged but found not guilty)
GILL	(AIDS)
PETE BEALE & girlfriend ROSE	(car crash, suspected foul play)
ARTHUR FOWLER	(heart attack)
LOU BEALE	(old age)
DEBBIE BATES	(hit by car)
ANDY O'BRIEN	(hero nurse hit by lorry saving child)
CHARLIE COTTON	(lorry crash)
DONNA LUDLOW	(drug overdose)
BABY HASSAN	(cot death)
TIFFANY MITCHELL	(run over by Frank Butcher)
CINDY BEALE	(died in childbirth)
SASKIA DUNCAN	(bashed over head with ashtray by Steve Owen)

What do you mean - 'Lost the plot!'

Mirror, mirror on the wall...

WEDDINGS

The national divorce rate may be high, but in Albert Square, there's more chance of *Hollyoaks* overtaking *EastEnders* in the ratings than a bride and groom reaching their silver anniversary.

Still, a wedding's always a good excuse for the ladies to go 'up West' to get a new outfit, and Frank to drool, 'you look the bees knees, darlin'...'

'For richer, for poorer, in sickness and in health, and until the scriptwriters decide it's over...'

PHIL MITCHELL AND KATHY BEALE

Love blossomed for Phil and Kathy after a trip to Paris, and they wed in a low-key registry office affair with just Pat and Grant as witnesses. That's Grant, as in the brother-in-law our blushing bride was later to find herself in a passionate clinch with...
(February '95)

LOFTY HOLLOWAY AND MICHELLE FOWLER

An early headline maker when 'Chelle climbed into her white meringue frock, but lost her bottle and jilted Lofty at the altar. The pair finally married in a quiet registry office do, but, *quelle surprise*, it didn't last.
(church in September '86)

Phil Collins joins cast as third Mitchell brother - shock

GRANT MITCHELL AND SHARON WATTS

A surprise Boxing Day wedding for Shazza. They'd barely had time to digest the cake when Grant's drunken rages and violent attacks drove her into the arms of brother Phil.
(December '91)

RICKY BUTCHER AND SAM MITCHELL

Walford's own Romeo and Juliet, the young couple eloped to Gretna Green with half the Square in hot pursuit. Even with Sam's bruvvers snapping at their heels, the teenage lovebirds managed to tie the knot.

IAN BEALE AND CINDY WILLIAMS

This doomed couple's wedding day was a taste of things to come. Scarlet woman Cindy wore red, an appropriate choice given that she was eight months pregnant by Simon Wicks. Things got off to a bad start with Cindy having a ding-dong with Ian and her new father-in-law Pete Beale. This was but a tiny glimpse of the misery of their life together.

GRANT MITCHELL AND TIFFANY RAYMOND

Tiff was up the duff with Grant's baby when they tied the knot in secret in Gibraltar. The following year, they got their marriage blessed, with Tiff looking so radiantly happy you just knew tragedy was around the corner.

PAT WICKS AND FRANK BUTCHER

Another big East End celebration for these aging lovebirds. They'd both been around the block a few times, but looked forward to a happy future together. Didn't they read the script?

Pass the spanner Rickeee

RICKY BUTCHER AND BIANCA JACKSON

More nail-biting nuptials, with Ricky marooned in a field in Kent with Grant and Phil after a wild, boozy stag night. The hapless trio hitched back to London while poor Bianca desperately circled the church in her bridal car. Married life with Rick-ayy proved to be equally aimless...
(April '97)

You won't find my wallet down there darlin'

Peggy Mitchell and Frank Butcher

Poor Pegs was only just out of hospital after surgery for breast cancer when she wed Frank. As befitted the elder statesmen of the square, there was a huge onscreen bash. The cast got in the swing of things, too, by having a party afterwards in a marquee in the Square.

NIGEL BATES AND DEBBIE TAYLOR

A surprise street party and merry knees-up for the wedding of nerdy Nigel to the bubbly Debbie. Nigel even forsook his usual explosion-in-a-paint-factory shirt-and-tie ensemble. Such happiness clearly couldn't last, and Nigel soon found himself on his lonesome once more – this time a grieving widower.

IRENE HILLS AND TERRY RAYMOND

Terry forgot to mention he was still married to first wife Louise, and did a runner from the first service. Eight months later, they married in a surprise ceremony after Terry told Irene they were going to see the bank manager.

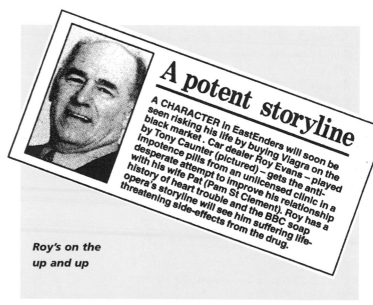

A potent storyline

A CHARACTER in EastEnders will soon be seen risking his life by buying Viagra on the black market . Car dealer Roy Evans – played by Tony Caunter (pictured) – gets the anti-impotence pills from an unlicensed clinic in a desperate attempt to improve his relationship with his wife Pat (Pam St Clement). Roy has a history of heart trouble and the BBC soap opera's storyline will see him suffering life-threatening side-effects from the drug.

Roy's on the up and up

Tiffany's all out of cheesey grins...

Peggy Butcher (Barbara Windsor)

Cor blimey! It's a brave man or woman that messes with Peggy Mitchell – part harridan, part pussycat, but all woman 'guvnor' of the Queen Vic. What's more, if she can't sort it, she knows a couple of lads that can. Cancer, dealing with thugs and putting up with Frank calling everyone darlin' – it's all in a day's work for our Peg. Even hard nut Grant knew he'd lost the plot when he dared lay a finger on his old mum. Down she may have been, but out? Never...

Babs Windsor may have a pretty hectic life on Albert Square, but the rucks, rows and romances she encounters as landlady of the Queen Vic and matriarch of the motley Mitchells aren't a patch on those that have made up her real life. *EastEnders* scriptwriters don't ever need to have to worry about storylines with our Babs in tow.

Born Barbara Ann Deeks in Shoreditch, east London, the only child of a bus conductor and a 'snobbish' dressmaker mother, her career took her from star of the London stage and nationwide celebrity to queen of the *Carry Ons* before suffering the indignity of regional panto and the threat of bankruptcy. She was even thinking about chucking in acting to become an agent.

That's before she was invited to join the cast of *EastEnders* in 1994 to fill the role of Peggy Mitchell, fearsome landlady of the Vic and moral guardian (some job) of Grant and Phil. It was an inspired spot of casting. Who other than Britain's best-loved actress could've filled Angie Watts' shoes so successfully after Anita Dobson called 'Time' on her stint behind the bar.

The role, of course, proved fairly timely for Babs – a useful lifeline back to the limelight where such a small but perfectly formed national institution as Barbara Windsor belongs. At just 4ft 10in in her stockinged feet, Babs's love life provides even greater entertainment than her career. After all, who else could follow a long line of East End gangsters, hoodlums and sharks by an equally long and unfeasible line in toyboys.

Babs's most high-profile relationship was with robber Ronnie Knight, though she claims not to have been aware of her husband's criminal tendencies throughout their 15 years together.

'He was good to me,'

she says. 'I was a little tart when I met him. I'd lost my virginity and was really acting disgracefully. Ronnie was a gent. He didn't look like a rogue, he was nice and polite and treated me like a lady.'

Babs says she did everything for her old man, from putting rollers in his hair, laying out his clothes with matching accessories for the day, and teaching him to read and write!

So when Ronnie asked her not to wear low-cut sweaters, she covered up her famous assets and smiled for the cameras alongside his pals (who just happened to include London underworld bosses the Krays) at a host of showbiz parties.

Even now, she won't slag off the Kray twins, saying Ronnie and Reggie treated her with respect. She even bedded their brother Charlie. 'He looked like Steve McQueen,' she explains. So that's all right, then.

The first time warning bells seemed to ring for our Babs was when she woke up one morning in 1984 to find that Ronnie had done a bunk to Spain. They divorced and he married Sue Haylock, who our heroine dismissed as 'a common barmaid'. Sue retaliated by calling her 'the peroxide dwarf', so clearly no love lost there.

After ten years Ronnie – apparently missing the food and weather – returned of his own accord to face the music over a string of crimes. He got seven years for his trouble.

Babs was prepared to forgive and forget, but then she read Ronnie's 1998 autobiography, *Memoirs and Confessions*. He claimed that Babs was a nymphomaniac who used to give him four blow jobs every morning, and dress up as Dick Whittington and Cinderella in the bedroom. ('A load of friggin lies!' she spluttered. 'I'd never have got into work...')

Worse, he also confessed that, though Babs had been his genuine alibi, he had

Facts

BABS wasn't allowed to show her belly button in the *Carry On* films.

BABS takes a dinky size 1 shoe.

27 MILLION people watched the first episode she appeared in. The actress was so nervous she kept throwing up on set.

BABS first trod the boards at Madame Behenna 's Juvenile Jollities dancing school.

Easy boy - or I'll have you for breakfast...

actually arranged the murder of a gangster called Alfredo Zomparelli in 1980.

'I couldn't believe that. I think that's terrible. I don't want to be a part of him now,' she says of the betrayal. Not such a gent now, eh Babs?

In between all this lowlife drama, our Babs managed to have a disastrous affair with *Carry On* co-star and comedy icon Sid James, despite the fact that they were both married to other people.

Though he wasn't your classic good-looker, Barbara says that women found Sid devastatingly attractive and was so in love with him she went to pieces when he died. 'I sobbed and sobbed and became sexually frigid.'

On screen, Peggy Mitchell's initial relationship didn't drift far from real life, but then it didn't need to, did it? With her husband Eric dead from cancer, Peg was open to offers. She fell for local Walford gangster George Palmer (gyms, gambling clubs and other clichés) but dumped him when she found out the extent of his dodgy deals. (Sound familiar?)

Wisely, George did a bunk to Spain, er, sorry, New Zealand to escape the wrath of Peggy and the rival gangster community. Meanwhile, reformed loser and down-and-out turned successful car dealer Frank Butcher stepped stealthily as an elephant into Peggy's affections and the flat above the pub.

He may not be everyone's idea of a good catch – after all, he did spend 18 months in psychiatric care – but

Kiss all you like - you'll never turn Frank into a handsome prince

Mummy's boy...

his never-ending supply of clichéd cockney wisdom won Peggy's heart.

The fact that Peg had just come out of hospital after a mastectomy operation put something of a dampener on their wedding, but the pair seem to be a match made in heaven, despite the fact that Frank accidentally killed Peggy's beloved daughter-in-law Tiff.

Babs is delighted by her screen husband, even though she only comes up to his navel. (Or perhaps that's why – she's never copped an eyeful of his scary set of gnashers.) 'You can't help but fancy Mike Reid,' she burbles. 'He's got this wonderful charisma.' Hmm...

And her screen happiness seems to be reflected in her current off-screen romances. After two failed long-term relationships with toyboys Stephen Hollings and Scott Harvey (Stephen, 20 years her junior, wouldn't have sex after the first year of marriage, while Scott, 25 years younger than her, was always up for a shag but had a drink problem), Babs, still fabulous at 61, is now dating two men closer to her own age.

Step forward, and stock up on the Viagra, restaurateur Robert Dunn, 50, and Scotland Yard detective Nigel Wildman, 52, of whom Babs reveals, 'He romanced me and made me feel like a woman again. Before, I wasn't getting sex and I do need it.

'I'm a real good bird to be with,' she adds. 'I make a fuss of the men in my life and run around them like a tit in a trance.'

She's a woman of the world too, hazarding a guess that she's slept with maybe a hundred men – 'but only because I've been around a long time!'

What Grant and Phil would make of all this is anyone's guess. But luckily their dear old mum isn't quite such a goer as our Babs. She's more interested in interfering in other people's affairs, pulling pints and doing a spot of shopping up West.

Gossip

BARBARA WINDSOR
(AKA PEGGY BUTCHER)

BABS never had kids, but doesn't think of Ross Kemp and Steve McFadden as the sons she never had – 'Nah! I fancy them both rotten!'

GAY *Carry On* star Kenneth Williams once proposed to her because she was the only woman he knew who cleaned her teeth after lunch. She turned him down when he said there'd be no sex.

SOCCER hardman turned actor Vinnie Jones is reported to be playing Ronnie Knight in a movie. Babs doesn't mind as long as her part isn't played by Sam Fox!

CHRIS EVANS may reckon that his campaign helped get Babs behind the Queen Vic bar but, spookily enough, she was already in negotiations with the show at the time.

OK so you don't like the wig, but I've still got more hair up one nostril than you two have on your heads

EASTENDER'S REPRIEVE

EASTENDERS star Peter Dean, who was facing the axe after reported bust-ups with writers and cast members, has been thrown a lifeline.

His character, barrow boy Pete Beale, was to have been killed off to coincide with Dean's contract ending this month. Instead, gangster's moll Rosie Chapman will survive a beating meant for him and the pair will make plans to flee together, leaving the way open for a comeback. New BBC1 programme controller Alan Yentob, who axed Eldorado, is believed to be behind the decision.

They always get you in the end

There's a rat in the kitchen -
Ian Beale

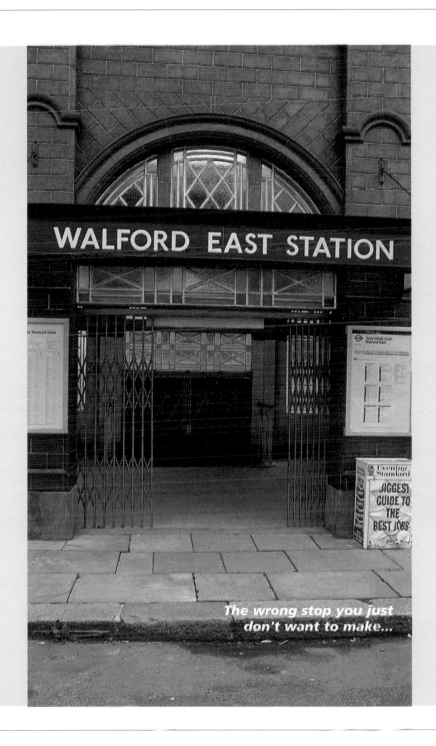

The wrong stop you just don't want to make...

Ross Kemp (aka Grant Mitchell)

Did you spill my pint? As far as welcoming pub landlords go, Grant was up there with Attila the Hun. Along with his equally follically-challenged bruv Phil, he likes nothing better than a good old ruck. And, with a list of enemies as long as his muscled arm, he's never short of takers.

His tight T-shirt proved a turn-on for more than one East End bird, but his love life suffered from his habit of giving them a knuckle sandwich before the courtship was through.

You'd reckon that after losing two wives Grant might've learned his lesson, but you obviously can't teach an old bulldog new tricks.

Hard bloke

New residents to Albert Square quickly realise the one simple rule when it comes to dealing with this volatile Mitchell brother – when the veins in his neck bulge and he starts cracking his knuckles, it's time to head for the door.

As his old schoolmate nerdy Nigel put it: 'Grant's only got three moods: happy, miserable and homicidal.'

Strangely, this neanderthal behaviour didn't bother the female population, even though going to bed with Grant should carry a Government Health Warning.

You'll never Adam and Eve it, but Ross Kemp couldn't be less like Grant in real life. Shockingly, he's more likely to be spotted sipping a fine wine with Peter Mandelson than mixing it with real East Enders. Yup, brace yourselves – Grunt is really a New Labour luvvie. He's even the Rector of Glasgow

University, for gawd's sake.

In fact, Ross is such a tree-hugger, it's a tribute to the man's acting skills that he's managed to be just such a menacing screen presence.

He was a jobbing actor specialising in hard-man roles when the call came through for *EastEnders*.

He and Phil first strode into view, oozing testosterone from every pore, in 1990, the pair of them making the perfect villainous duo to replace Dirty Den. Handy with his fists, and eager to 'sort it', Grant ruled the Square with a rod of iron.

In ten years, Grant's menacing presence has struck terror into the heart of more than one wife. He even clocked his beloved mum Peggy one during a row, but somehow just never made time for that anger management course.

Sensitive Ross never wanted to be the ultimate screen thug,

though. He got the programme-makers to axe the planned rape of Tiffany on Christmas Day 1997, saying he'd rather quit. 'I didn't think it was particularly festive,' he commented. The boy's got a point really.

And, though his behaviour drove her to an all too early grave, Ross refused to be Tiffany's murderer. So poor old Frank drew the short straw instead, leaving the door open for Ross's return.

All this violence couldn't be more alien to Ross. But that didn't stop some not-so-bright gangland bosses getting their fact confused with fiction in 1999, when it was reported that there was a contract out to maim Ross for being a grass.

The villains offered £500 for anyone willing to break the actor's legs because they believed he'd shopped *London's Burning* star John Alford, jailed for supplying cocaine. Police advised Ross not to go drinking on his

Gossip

ROSS KEMP (AKA GRANT MITCHELL)

ROSS is a big fan of the old *Carry On* films.

BOTH he and Steve McFadden (who plays Phil) were up for the part of Grant.

HIS showbiz break was playing a munchkin in a 1985 panto *Wizard of Oz*. He got £100 per week – a bit more than the £120,000 pa he earned on EastEnders.

BELIEVE it or not, his first TV break came via a minor part in another long-running British soap – Emmerdale. He also popped up in *Birds of a Feather* and *The Manageress*.

TALK about a change of character – Ross played a transvestite on BBC cop drama *City Central*. He looked a treat, and said, 'I loved doing something different.'

own – but can Phil be trusted in a boozer these days?

Unlike a lot of *EastEnders* stars, Ross prefers to stay out of the tabloids, but isn't afraid of sleeping with the enemy – his on/off girlfriend, Rebekah Wade, is deputy editor of *The Sun*.

So where does Grant's awesome aggression come from? Ross based the character on people he'd known, saying there are a lot of Grants around. 'My grandad was a very strong domineering man and I've taken

some of that.'

A psychologist wouldn't have to look too far to find out just why Grant is so grumpy. It stems back to a traumatic experience as an 18-year-old squaddie fighting in the Falklands War when Grant shot an unarmed Argentinian soldier dead. Ever since, he's had nightmares from which he wakes screaming.

Oh, that and the fact that his ex-boxer dad was a violent drunk, womaniser and a gambler who used Grant – a skinny, gentle kid, by all accounts – as

Soft bloke

a punchbag when he came home pissed of an evening. Nice choice, Peggy.

The younger by a year and a half, Grant made a childhood pact with his brother Phil to protect each other, no matter what. Which would account for them closing ranks when the chips are down.

The shaven-headed pair had barely set up their auto repair shop in the Arches (paid for with a gambling win of Phil's) before they'd cornered the market in doing up stolen cars and forging MOT certificates.

Known, not so affectionately as Tweedledum and Tweedledee when they first arrived, the bruvvers soon made their presence felt. Grant set his cap at buxom blonde Sharon, who really should've been deafened by the sound of warning bells clanging when he hospitalised ex-bent copper, Eddie Royle when wooing her.

This mindless violence was to become

There's no way I'm going out with you looking like that Tiff...

an all-too-familiar mating ritual of Grant's, but, though Shazza had her doubts, she agrees to marry him when he says he'll get back the Queen Vic for her. (This a woman for whom the stained carpet and nicotine-yellow ceiling are more appealing than any royal palace.)

One gun siege and a fire which nearly kills her later, Shaz has had enough of her hubby's brutish ways, and turns to Phil in the 1994 Sharongate saga. When Grant discovered that the two people he loved most had betrayed him, there was little he could do, after he'd put his

bruv in hospital, but cry.

'I'm not the sort of person who cries easily, so I had a flood of tears stored up,' reveals Ross. 'It was probably good for me to get rid of them all.'

Showing that Grant had a soft side made Ross realise how seriously the nation took the soap.

'I was so used to people having a go at me, I found it amazing that they started telling me not to worry,' he says. 'I once went past a fish shop and the owner came out and gave me a whole sea bass!'

After Shaz flounced out for a new life, Grant managed to get Michelle pregnant during a drunken one-nighter, but hooked up with Tiff when she offered him the chance of parenthood.

Grant seemed to have a problem with the concept of fidelity though, moving in on Northern temptress Lorraine Wicks, his mum-in-law Louise and sister-in-law Kath. Though she didn't do much for her chances of survival, saying of Sharon: 'I always thought she was rather fat.' Oh dear...

Leaving the Vic to go into business with Steve Owen, Grant still couldn't tear himself away from his dear old mum or Phil – the brothers even started wearing a nice line in matching button-down shirts.

But his love life started to look distinctly dodgy again when he started wooing barmaid Nina, a gal with a past.

IT'S A FACT!

THERE ARE TWO REAL ALBERT SQUARES IN LONDON, ONE IN STRATFORD E15 AND ONE IN WANDSWORTH SW8

If she takes the hat off - run - it means she's going to sing....

Martine McCutcheon (Tiffany Mitchell)

Poor tragic Tiff. From bouncy barmaid to battered wife to corpse, she was proof that marrying a Mitchell brother can be very bad for your health. But the girl only had herself to blame. Having gone all out to ensnare Grant, knowing he didn't really love her, it shouldn't have come as any great surprise when he started playing away from home. And while she saw off Northern love rival Lorraine, Tiffany forgot the golden rule of soaps: Trust no one, not even your own mother.

Tiffany may have led the life of a victim, but actress Martine McCutcheon is made of sterner stuff. A real East Ender, she was born in Hackney and brought up in a succession of dingy flats by her mum Jenny who left her street trader dad Thomas Hemmings when Martine was just two.

This tough early life sowed the seeds of ambition. Jenny had three jobs – cleaning, working in a building society and as a barmaid, but, whenever they could, Martine and her mum would settle down in front of their one precious possession, an old black and white telly with a coathanger for an aerial.

While her mates were listening to Duran Duran, Martine was watching old movies and musicals, copying stars like Diana Ross and Barbra Streisand by doing shows in the front room in home-made costumes.

At seven, she was even reading the actor's

Nah, everyone up West wears them - they're suffisty wot yer call it cated...

MARTINE MCCUTCHEON (AKA TIFFANY MITCHELL)

MARTINE belted out the Phil Collins song 'Against All Odds', dressed in a gold lamé catsuit for her stage school audition. Amazingly, she got in!

HER ideal man is Frank Sinatra. 'I loved it when men were men and women were women. Now it's hard to tell what's what.'

MARTINE's new best friend is rich socialite shopper and reformed cokehead, Tara Palmer-Tompkinson.

MARTINE was pictured on a Labour Party poster aged six weeks, and was a Pears girl at five years old.

SHE was once voted sexiest woman in soap

trade paper, and knew that the glamorous world of showbiz was her escape route.

Ever since she had danced along to the TV show *Fame* in a green bikini, Martine had yearned to go to a performing arts school. Her mum wrote to more than 200 charities pleading with them to sponsor her daughter and, at ten years old, Martine got into the Italia Conti school.

Martine was on her way and, at 16, she joined three-girl pop band Milan. But five flop singles later, their biggest claim to fame was supporting East 17.

Life for this wannabe starlet was proving tough, and when she got the call from *EastEnders*, Martine was working in Knickerbox in Lakeside shopping centre for £1.50 an hour.

At first, the producers weren't sure if she was tarty enough to play Tiffany, so Martine marched back in wearing a short skirt, fishnet stockings, orange lipstick, fake tan and attitude. The part was hers.

It was a role she was born to play. As Tiffany, Martine blossomed from Bianca's slutty friend to a national treasure.

Finding herself pregnant and not knowing who the dad was, Tiff took a chance on Grant. (At the time, he seemed a better choice than drug dealer Tony Hills, especially after she caught him in a clinch with her gay brother Simon.)

Strangely, Tiff really fell for Grant, though their idea of foreplay was to swop tales of being beaten up by their dads. She even confessed that she got pregnant by a teacher when she was a teenager, but lost the baby when her loutish father, Terry Raymond, pushed her downstairs. (You shouldn't give a bloke ideas, Tiff, sweetheart.)

Tiff's plucky sweetness grew on Grant, and he softened enough after the birth of Courtney to make an honest women of her. She trained as an aromaferapist/masseuse and, for a few brief months, it looked like the pair had put a dysfunctional childhood behind them and were going to make a go of it.

But tragedy loomed when long-suffering Tiff learned of his fling with her floozy mum Louise and walked out taking baby Courtney. They argued and Tiffany, probably wishing she'd moved into a bungalow, was sent tumbling down the stairs for the second time in her short life.

White-faced, hair askew and hooked up to a life support machine, Martine did a good coma. But in a brutal plot twist, she revived, only to be mown down by Frank (Butcher by name, butcher by nature).

So farewell, then Tiffany/Martine. For millions of viewers, seeing you on *Top Of The Pops* singing your No 1 hit 'Perfect Moment' was more of a tragic moment. How could you turn your back on being a soap star to go for a million pound record deal to become a pop princess? Has Kylie's career taught you nothing?

But Martine says she always planned to use *EastEnders* as a stepping stone to music. 'I want to try everything. I don't want to get to 60 and look back and say 'I wish...'

Louise, your face has dropped

Classic Tiffany quotes

'COURTNEY LOVES THE TELETUBBIES BECAUSE TINKY WINKY LOOKS LIKE GRANT'

Facts

Two endings were shot – one showing Tiff bleeding to death on the pavement, the other showing her leaving, alive and well, in a taxi...

THE first Martine heard about Tiffany's death was on the car radio. She'd quit the series hoping she could return, and was heartbroken to discover she was being killed off.

'I've told you, Gillian, that is not where I keep my sausage'

Adam Woodyatt (aka Ian Beale)

to outrageous behaviour was being branded a 'neighbour from hell' for merely mowing his lawn on a Sunday afternoon!

How very, very different from Ian's rollercoaster ride through life. He went from an amiable schoolboy to a ruthless yuppie for no clear reason, though perhaps being married to scheming Cindy could've had something to do with it.

So smitten was he by this bleached-haired temptress, he put up with her unfaithfulness, desertion and insults, but drew the line when he found out she'd hired a hitman to bump him off.

Bizarrely, he paid classic tribute to Cindy's 'loving and funny'

Cindy Peel – the avenger

Playing Ian Beale since you were barely out of short trousers could do strange things to an actor, but Adam Woodyatt seems happily free of any of the irritating traits that have made Albert Square's yuppie tycoon such an all-round pain in the arse.

Shy and retiring by nature, Adam is more interested in laying a patio than partying.

He started earning money doing TV commercials when he was just seven and, at 16, got the part in *EastEnders* and moved out into his own place.

He and long-time girlfriend Beverley Sharp married in 1998 in Disney World, Florida, and live quietly in Warwickshire with their two small children, avoiding the scandal that has dogged other stars. The closest he got personality at her funeral. 'Just think of the good times, the happy memories,' he said. That'd be a two second silence then.

But however turbulent his private life, Ian always found time to make a few quid and, like any master of the Universe, this Albert Square business mogul just doesn't care who he tramples over in his rise to the top. (You can tell he's a yuppie because he wears a mackintosh, uses a mobile phone and occasionally sports a wispy moustache.)

And though they're not exactly glamourous career choices – a fish and chip shop and bargain basement shop – he's always got some new money-making scheme on the go, which doesn't hurt his chances with mega-babe Melanie.

Gossip

ADAM WOODYATT (AKA IAN BEALE)

ADAM's a big *Star Trek* fan who enjoys playing cricket and golf.

HIS local Indian restaurant owner loves *EastEnders*, and always wants to know what's going to happen next. 'When I was shot and wouldn't tell him if I'd live or die, he said, 'Right, no curry!' says Adam.

REMEMBER when Ian was shot and was lying on pavement with his guts spilling out, *Reservoir Dogs*-style? Well, he had to stay very still between takes, because the fake blood was made of Fairy Liquid and red dye, and if he moved too quickly it frothed up into shiny bubbles.

Get real about health, doctor tells soaps

TV's smoking and drinking characters 'look much too fit'

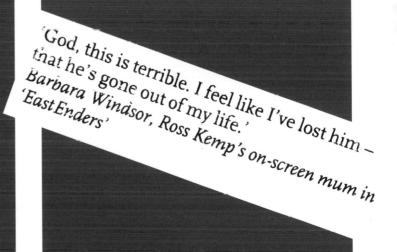

'God, this is terrible. I feel like I've lost him – that he's gone out of my life.'
Barbara Windsor, Ross Kemp's on-screen mum in 'EastEnders'

You're better off living in Baghdad

Look's like Rickeee's taken a wrench to Bianca's Barnet

Patsy Palmer (aka Bianca Butcher)

Missing you already (not). The residents of Albert Square bade a delighted farewell to the ginger whinger, a girl who'd given them all the sharp end of her tongue at one time or another. But it was no wonder Bianca looked permanently pissed off. Life had a nasty habit of kicking her full in the freckles. Only 22, she'd already lived through enough drama to fill ten Oprah shows – a mum who changed her fellas on a weekly basis, finding out that the bloke she fancied was actually her dad, then losing her baby. And, though her Ricky meant well, somehow hunky Dan was more of a man than he could ever be.

'Rick-ayyy!' That familiar resounding cry is no more, and Walford is a far quieter place after the departure of Bianca, a girl for whom a day without mouthing off was a day wasted.

And while actress Patsy Palmer reckons the British public will be glad to see the back of B's tantrums, she credits *EastEnders* with saving her from a life that was shaping up to being just as miserable as her character's.

She'd been a star pupil at the Anna Scher theatre school but, at 19, Patsy was a single mum, living with her baby son Charley in a freezing flat in a rough part of Bethnal Green, east London. She had no money and no work apart from a few bit parts in *The Bill*.

Depressed, she threw herself into the rave drug scene, partying on cocaine and ecstasy.

Then, when Charley was 18 months old, she got the part of Bianca, and says that having money for the first time in her life made her well.

But her problems weren't all over, and Patsy, who admits she has an addictive personality, found herself battling anorexia, her weight falling to seven stone.

'My problem went from drink to drugs to food. I could almost get a high when I wasn't eating,' she says. 'I felt life would be all right if I was skinny – I look back now and think I was mad.'

Shut it Bianca, everyone can beat Robbie

Counselling sessions helped, and she blames her lack of confidence on her childhood.

'I grew up feeling so insecure. I looked like a little fishfinger at school and all the kids would jeer at me and call me Gingernut. Girls would push me up against the wall and tell me how ugly I was.'

Prettier than she appears onscreen, Patsy started dating film producer Nick Love and, after an on/off love affair, they got married in true tabloid-style in a registry office with just four pals and seven minders as guests – she'd sold the rights to *OK* magazine. The couple split six months later, and now she's with cabbie Richard Merkell.

But it was as rottweiler-chewing-a-lemon Bianca that was Patsy's finest hour. Whether it was having a full-on tantrum at long-suffering hubby Ricky or merely suffering in mute, sulky silence, Bianca was not a happy bunny.

Gossip

PATSY PALMER (AKA BIANCA BUTCHER)

PATSY's real name is Julie Harris.

HER son Charley goes to a private school.

SHE still lives in Bethnal Green, but these days it's in a posh terraced house.

PATSY apparently plans to go to elocution lessons 'to learn how to speak posh'.

HER brother Albert was hooked on heroin and crack cocaine and served a three-year sentence for burglary. Patsy, who is now patron of drug charity Action on Addiction, sent fellow inmates signed photos of herself.

PATSY is five years older than her screen character.

Perhaps mum Carol's succession of blokes had made her cynical about men, but then, she did have a fair bit to be miserable about. First she came on strong to David Wicks, only to discover he was really her dad. He disappeared out of her life again, then she found out her so-called friend Natalie had slept with Ricky. She had to abort her baby, and her best mate Tiffany died.

It was no life for a girl, and when muscly Dan, who she'd had a fling with at 15, turned up, poor B became so pale her lips almost disappeared.

When they finally snog (just after he's proposed to her mum), she has the look of a stunned mullet.

Even baby Liam, the love of Ricky and her market stall, BB's Fashions, aren't enough. The girl's gotta get out of the Square and get a life – but, as Patsy hasn't ruled out coming back, stand by for that familiar war cry again ...'Rick-ayyy!'.

Love strikes at the most unexpected moments

"Yeah, the Viagr
certainly working.

Oh, Oh, here's trouble...

Danniella Morgan
(aka Samantha Mitchell)

Lock up your fellas – she's back! Sam's modelling career didn't exactly give Kate and Naomi sleepless nights, and she's only pint-sized, but when it comes to causing trouble, Sam's got it sussed. A teen bride who broke ex-husband Ricky's heart, she knows that big brothers Phil and Grant are always there to sort out anyone who takes advantage. But, really, she don't need 'em. Because if anyone can look after themselves, it's Sam.

For Danniella Westbrook (as she was known then), the uncrowned queen of the Essex girls, life was a soap opera to be played out on the front pages of the press. But it's a dangerous game, and her *EastEnders* fame and fortune nearly destroyed her life. Her telly antics as Ricky's wayward child bride were nothing on what she got up to offscreen.

She joined the soap in 1990 at just 16, and milked her celeb status from the start. She was a regular at every showbiz bash, but it was when she met East 17 singer Brian Harvey a few years later that her partying got out of control.

The white stiletto brigade's answer to Richard Burton and Elizabeth Taylor, the couple had a tempestuous affair, played out in various glitzy nightspots 'up West'. Forever being snapped by the paparazzi staggering drunkenly out on to the street in the early hours of the morning, Danniella and Brian were a gift to the tabloids.

She favoured the timelessly classic style of big hair, skin-tight micro-mini and cropped tops, while Brian was often hard to spot flapping aimlessly around inside over-sized baggy jackets and trousers.

Their tacky style reached its peak with the revelation that they'd joined the Mile High Club with a romp in a plane's toilet (and a hammock, a Jacuzzi, the sea and a steam room... yeah, yeah, we get the picture), and their

Like butter wouldn't melt in her mouth

Mr & Mrs Pepperpot

announcement on *The Big Breakfast* they were getting married. She was 21, he was 19.

But there was an even seedier side to this B-list love story. By now, Danniella was hooked on cocaine, blowing £100,000 on a two-year drug binge.

Things got so bad that, in October 1994, she wrote a suicide note and swallowed a cocktail of sleeping pills and painkillers. Luckily Brian found her and called an ambulance. With the help of therapy at a clinic, she beat her addiction and cleaned up her act, saying cocaine had ruined her life.

Kicked out of the soap for her drug abuse, Danniella also had a very public (natch) and bitter break-up with Brian Harvey. ('She's barking mad. Off her trolley,' he said later.)

Her acting career on the skids, she was spotted selling goods at a car boot sale and also working for a mobile phone company in Loughton Essex.

Then, in 1996, aged 22, Danni fell pregnant. But even the birth of baby son Kai didn't stop the headlines coming thick and fast, and more disaster struck when she and Kai were involved in a near-fatal car crash in 1998. Danniella nearly lost an eye, and her then-lover Robert Fernandez was later convicted of driving while banned.

Having lived life in the fast lane for so long, it seemed like Danniella was finally settling down when, in October 1998, she married baby-faced Ben Morgan, a courier she'd met at a petrol station just seven weeks earlier.

Gossip

DANNIELLA MORGAN (AKA SAMANTHA MITCHELL)

DANNIELLA first rolled on to the show as an extra – aged 11, on roller skates.

THE actress hates her lips and would like a collagen injection. She reckons her boobs are a bit on the small side too, but she likes her hair.

FORGET personality. Danniella goes for looks. 'I really appreciate good-looking men. No Mr Beans for me, thanks!'

DANNI's tight-lipped about the father of her baby, leading to a bizarre rumour that it could even be screen hunk Paul Nicholls's. 'One day I'll reveal who Kai's dad is, and, believe me, people will be shocked,' is all she'll say. So far.

And, though cynics sniggered, Danniella felt confident enough to tell the moving tale of their love, not once, but three times in *Hello!*.

The young couple headed to Australia for a new life, but forget Down Under, Danni's natural habitat is Walford. When the call came through that she could return to the soap, she was straight on the phone to Quantas, saying it was her dream come true. Let's just hope she doesn't blow it this time.

It all makes her life onscreen seem rather tame, really. So, Sam eloped to Gretna Green with Ricky, then disappeared to Spain for three years. But, apart from working in a dodgy nightclub, sleeping with casanova David Wicks and doing a bunk with Tiff's Spanish boyfriend when she popped back with her brothers in 1996, Sam has led a model existence compared to Danni's.

Maybe the scriptwriters should ask her for a few ideas...

Awards dinner? More like dog's dinner....

Steve McFadden (aka Phil Mitchell)

From lovable ruddy-faced lummox to alcoholic brute, Phil underwent a horrifying personality change. Maybe it was guilt at shagging Sharon, or the pressure of parenthood, but Phil took up residence in the gutter, making poor Kathy's life a misery and crying like a baby if you took away his bottle. He's sobered up, but while he's usually seen in the Vic nursing an orange juice, he's still not a man to be messed with.

Just five years old when he told his mum he was going to make the name McFadden famous, Steve had a feeling something big was going to happen in his life.

Born in 1959 in Maida Vale, West London, he was the only child in a close-knit family. His dad was a market trader and Steve was a bit of a rebel at school, getting into trouble for bunking off and swearing.

When he left school, Steve sold fake perfume and jewellery on Oxford Street and got caught up in petty crime.

He doesn't regret his dodgy past, and says he uses those experiences when he's playing Phil. In fact, like the Mitchells, he puts a lot of his troubles down to a bad attitude towards authority. 'I've done nothing to be ashamed of. I did stuff that loads of other kids do, but I was never very good at handling the police. I wound them up.'

Out of the blue, at 25, Steve applied to top drama school, RADA. 'I wasn't vain, but I did have a deep sense of self-belief. Everyone is talented – it's just a question of channelling your talents.'

His confidence paid off, and he won a place alongside Ralph (*The English Patient*) Fiennes, though their careers moved in slightly different directions when Steve found himself barrelling down the usual tough-looking London actor's route of thugs in *The Bill*, *Bergerac* and *Minder*.

Wary of the press, Steve likes to keep his private life private, but found himself on the front pages in 1992 when he was reported to have checked into a clinic to help him overcome his drink addiction and then a couple of years later when he was viciously attacked by a deranged tramp at London's Waterloo Bridge.

The vagrant apparently yelled, 'Who do you think you are, Grant Mitchell?' before slashing him so badly he had to have 50 stitches.

In his private life, Steve's passion is cars and keeping in shape with regular sessions with punchbag and rowing machine. He's even got a mini-gym at his North London home.

'My tool is my body and I have to look after it,' he says in a very un-Phil-like way.

Steve likes to drive a Rolls-Royce, but keeps a fleet of cars, vans and motorbikes. When he was banned for drink-driving in 1996, he cycled around with a cap on so he wouldn't get recognised.

With a teenage son Matt by childhood sweetheart Sue, plus a daughter Teona born in 1997 to girlfriend Angela Bostock, Steve's never been married. 'It doesn't do a lot for me. It's just getting tangled up with the law,' he reckons.

Phil would probably agree. After a marriage of convenience with Romanian refugee, Nadia, he proposed to Kath. At the time, apart from accidentally

Both brothers regularly attend SA meetings - Slapheads Anonymous

Duke of Albert Square

AT the Queen Vic, the only excuse would be a fancy dress bash. But EastEnder Grant Mitchell — alias Ross Kemp — doesn't appear to be in party mood in his period costume and wig. The actor, looking more familiar below, posed as the Duke of Buckingham to present a feature for the BBC's historical documentary series One Foot in the Past, on Cliveden, the Berkshire house built by the Duke. Kemp fell in love with Cliveden, former home of Lady Astor, while appearing there in a drama school production.

That Regaine really seems to work...

burning a man to death when he set fire to Frank's car lot for the insurance dosh, Phil doesn't seem to be too bad a bet.

A generally good-natured bloke (if you can ignore the odd murder), he was more reasonable than his brother, happy with the odd pint. Then, almost overnight, he turned into a violent alcoholic, barely able to string two words together.

Understandably confused to find herself sharing a bed with a care in the community candidate, Kaff decided she'd had enough, leaving Phil free to get involved with Annie Palmer and a protection racket.

These days, our chunky, garage-owning hard nut is nearly back to his old, calmer self, even stepping in to rescue godson Jamie from his drunk, violent uncle (er, pot and kettle, anyone?). But, having glimpsed his major potential for nastiness, it'd be a brave woman who'd take him on.

Bummer, it's tickets for two

And, don't forget, this is the devoted brother who slept with Sharon, the love of Grant's life.

Not surprisingly, Steve reckons he's smarter than his character Phil. 'I've got a few more brain cells, and I don't think I would find myself in a lot of the situations he finds himself in. But I would have him as a mate. I like him. And I'd definitely get him to fix my cars...'

Classic Grant quote

'KATHY'S AN OBG – AN OLDIE BUT A GOODIE. THOUGH IT'S A BIT OF A DISAPPOINTMENT WHEN SHE'S GOT HER KIT OFF. NOTHING PERSONAL, KATH'

Gossip

STEVE McFADDEN (AKA PHIL MITCHELL)

ACCORDING to their hairdresser, Steve has more hair than Ross Kemp.

A MUSIC lover who loves Led Zeppelin and New Order, you might trip over Steve's tent when he goes camping out at Glastonbury.

HE likes going fishing and has a house and speedboat in Cornwall.

THE young Steve was a bit of a Brando fan.

SUEDE singer Brett Anderson once dreamed about robbing a bank with Phil.

STEVE sang on the title track of Babs Windsor's LP 'You've Got a Friend' and says he fancies his screen mum. 'She's gorgeous.'

Wearing clothes made of curtain material might be OK. Putting chandeliers in your ears isn't.

Pam St Clement (aka Pat Evans)

With her livid blue eye shadow, pearly pink lippy and chandelier earrings, Pat may have a drag queen's sense of style, but that still doesn't stop blokes of a certain age fighting for her affections. In fact, as the EastEnder who's least like her character, actress Pam actually came out as a lesbian in 1990.

Her mum died when she was a child, and Pam spent most of her childhood at boarding school. She married Royal Navy Marine Engineer Andrew Gordon, but the couple didn't have children.

After working as a school teacher, Pam's acting break came in the 1970s prison drama Within These Walls. She had a 17-year relationship with partner Jackie Reed which finished in 1994.

Jackie suffered from ME, and Pam believes that the illness was brought on by the stress of coping with the press intrusion into their life: 'Being a celebrity isn't always a lot of fun,' she adds.

No longer 'Fat Pat', Pam has recently lost five stone, slimming down from size 22 to size 14. She celebrated by filling six bin liners with old clothes, taking them to a charity shop and buying a pair of leather trousers. Now she's a new woman, saying, 'I feel like a 16-year-old inside.'

I have loads of friends and many are a lot younger than me. The age barrier doesn't have to exist. I love dancing and bopping around.'

To be honest, the thought of Pat Evans bopping around is too scary to contemplate.

Since she first appeared in 1986 in a floral chiffon frock, her dress sense had gone downhill fast.

The woman's been round the block a few times, too. Married to Frank Butcher (who bedded her at 16 after she won a Butlin's beauty contest), Pete Beale, and now poor, impotent Roy, Pat has mellowed from aging slapper into the robust and reliable fount of all wisdom.

As a mother she's a bit of a dead loss, though, and never hears from her boys

Roy begining to wish Viagra hadn't been invented

Simon and David. Like her ex-hubby Frank, she's not too clever behind the wheel of a car either, having been jailed for six months after killing a teenager in her cab after a few G&Ts too many.

Pam reckons Pat'll be around for a good few years to come too. 'I like the fact she is a survivor. I'm not sure I am. If the boat was going down, I think I'd say, "Oh sod it, I'll go down with it".'

Gossip

PAM ST CLEMENTS
(AKA PAT EVANS)

A LOT of Pat's earrings are sent in by fans.

PAM had a narrow escape from a lion and a deadly Mamba spider on safari in Africa, but would still love to present a TV show about wildlife.

SHE takes loads of Vitamin C to keep her energy up.

Tony Caunter (aka Roy Evans)

Quite what Roy sees in Pat is a mystery to viewers – and to the actor who plays him. In their first scene together she has a go at him for selling her boy David a dodgy motor. 'Roy was instantly attracted to Pat, though I'll never understand why,' says Tony.

A semi-successful businessman (well, he wears a suit which makes him slightly higher up the evolutionary scale than most of his neighbours) who spends most of his life babying son Barry, Walford hasn't been kind to Roy. A heart attack at Christmas 1998, he also attempted suicide when a business deal went wrong.

Now he's stuck in partnership with Frank selling cars at Deals on Wheels, and still married to Pat, even though he's not been delivering in the bedroom.

The impotence storyline was considered pretty raunchy for such early evening viewing, but was all handled in the best possible taste – unlike Pat's outfits.

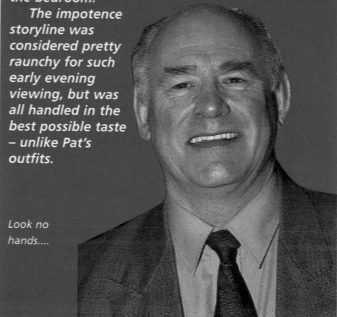

Look no hands....

'Bianca, this is what happens if you don't look after your clothes properly'

Makes Nigel look like Richard Gere

Shaun Williamson (aka Barry Evans)

The grown-up son who acts like a big girl's blouse, Barry is a classic spoilt only child. He acted as go-between for Cindy and her hit man, then fell for scheming Vanessa who ran off with all the money from the car business, causing Bazza to end up in the dumping ground for losers – the squat.

And when he found out that his dad had cheated on his mum, he went into such a giant sulk even the long-suffering Roy lost patience with him.

Now running dating agency Romantic Relations with Natalie (who had unaccountably been sharing his bed as well as his office space) he has the look of a permanently worried man.

Actor Shaun is much more sorted. Married with a baby daughter, he's a man of many talents. He worked as a Bluecoat, shelf-stacker and an accountant in the Navy, and also has a second career as a crooner. You can often hear him belting out classics like 'Young Girl' and 'Love Train' on the London cabaret circuit.

Classic Barry quote

'I'VE GOT AN EXPANDING WAISTLINE AND A RETREATING FOREHEAD'

Albert Square

Bowing out: Kemp as Mitchell, with Tiffany

By OLIVER HARVEY Showbusiness Reporter

EastEnders star Ross Kemp has been poached by ITV in a £1.2million deal. The 34-year-old actor, who played Grant Mitchell for ten years, will film his last scenes in Albert Square in August. 'EastEnders has provided me with an excellent opportunity to develop my acting skills,' he said. 'I now look forward to new challenges and expanding my range as an actor.

'I'm going to miss playing Grant. You could say we've been through a lot together – two marriages, a divorce, countless affairs (including the mother-in-law), children, prison, endless fights and a lot of crying.'

Capturing Kemp, one of the BBC's biggest stars, is a huge coup for ITV. The two-year golden handcuffs deal will give him double what the BBC paid him for 11 hours of peak-time drama. Projects include Active Defence, a major new series covering notorious miscarriages of justice in which he is lined up to

'End will be dramatic but not final'

play a lawyer. He will play a security guard who finds a sack full of money in a two-hour special called Hero Of The Hour. His character is faced with the dilemma of whether to keep the cash to pay for a vital operation for his sick daughter. Hardman Mitchell has been involved in some of EastEnders' most notorious plots. In 1992 he set fire to the Queen Vic in an attempted insurance scam. A year later it emerged his brother had been having an affair with his wife. Scriptwriters now have to decide how to write him out, but have pledged he will not be killed off like his screen wife Tiffany, played by Martine McCutcheon, who was run over by a car. Instead he will be at the centre of a plot line that will take him away from Albert Square but allow the chance of a return.

'There will always be a pint waiting on the bar of the Queen Vic for Grant,' executive producer Matthew Robinson said. 'Grant's exit will be dramatic but not final.' Kemp said. 'I think I will have some say in the way Grant is written out because my departure has been so amicable.' ITV director of programmes David Liddiment said: 'Ross has built up an amazing relationship with the British public. I am absolutely thrilled he is coming to ITV to extend that relationship.'

Ross looks forward to more sensitive roles on ITV - like the Marquis de Sade, and Attila the Hun

Cheer up Mike - things could be worse...

Mike Reid (aka Frank Butcher)

It's a funny old world, innit? Who would've thought a few years back that Frank would end up happily pulling pints behind the Queen Vic bar with a lovely lady by his side?

Once married to Pat, his life went further downhill when he cracked up after the death of a vagrant on his car lot. He'd got Phil to torch the place for the insurance wedge and, unable to cope, he disappeared and spent 18 months in psychiatric care. But, like a bad penny, he turned up back in Walford and was soon moving in on Peggy.

Now firmly established as your regular nightmare cockney landlord, Frank just can't resist the chance to churn out a cliché to the punters.

A gent of the old school, he calls everyone 'sweetheart', smiling his scary smile. Strangely, Peg seems rather taken with his big white teeth and thin lips, and doesn't even shudder at that horrible guttural voice, perhaps because he's good for her ego, forever telling her she looks 'like a million dollars, sweetheart'.

Marriage seems to have put an end to Frank's duckin' and divin' for the time being, but as The Butcher of Walford, responsible for two deaths, tragedy can only be just around the corner.

In fact, Mike Reid's own life has had its share of trauma that even the scriptwriters couldn't come up with.

Married to Shirley since he was 18, the couple had three children, but tragedy struck when his son Mark

Told you.

Gossip

MIKE REID
(AKA FRANK BUTCHER)

MIKE Reid was once a Hackney coalman.

FRANK'S character appeared because the producers wanted to show that even a tough old bird like Pat had once really loved someone.

HE wasn't happy about the show going from two episodes a week to three. 'But at the end of the day we're all lucky to be in work,' he said, realistically.

accidentally killed his best friend in a shooting accident.

Four years later, still overwhelmed by guilt and remorse, Mark committed suicide. He and his girlfriend Annette were the parents of Kirsty Anne and Michael and, four months after the suicide, Kirsty Anne became a cot death victim.

Mike was on the set of *EastEnders* when he heard the terrible news, but after comforting Shirley he carried on filming.

'I had to,' he says, 'there were 200 people out there relying on me. I just done my job and when I'd finished I went out and had a good cry.'

The son of a lorry driver, Mike never trained as an actor, starting life telling gags as the skinhead comic on *The Comedians*. He still does comedy gigs when he gets the chance. 'It's like a holiday to me. If I don't get onstage I get withdrawal symptoms,' he says.

He loves playing Frank, though, and identifies with his character. 'Frank's not a bad old boy. He's pretty similar to me in lots of ways.

'I've been up and down so many times. I've had a very rich life. Some aspects I could've done without, but I've got a lot to be thankful for. I still keep bobbing back.'

Little big voice

Barbara Windsor
You've Got a Friend (Telstar)
★★★★

Come on - you've slept with everyone else

Soap Rule No 1:

Never let showb

your head

Hair today, gone tomorrow.

Yes, that's right, Bianca, pull your draws up, luv

No Sid, honest - you look great...

Sid Owen (aka Ricky Butcher)

He'll never make the *Mastermind* finals, but if you're a single girl with a car wot needs fixing, then Ricky's your man. He'll have your big end sorted and be waltzing you down the aisle before you can say, 'Is VAT included?'
Still only in his twenties, he's been married twice – seems Albert Square's long-standing grease monkey just can't get by without a trouble-and-strife to make his life miserable.

For a simple sort of bloke, Ricky's got a pretty complicated love life. First there was Sam, but she legged it abroad to be a top international model (not). Then old misery guts Bianca, whose mission in life seemed to be to make his life more depressing than it already was.

Still, he's a good sort, old Ricky – he ain't got a bad word to say about anyone. And there's always the sanctuary of the Arches when woman worries get him down – though if Phil's your idea of a port in a storm you've got trouble.

But if Ricky is happy with the simple life, actor Sid Owen is rather more sophisticated. He's certainly got better taste in birds, and since his split with stunning long-term girlfriend model Lucy Braybrook, he's been linked with Nicole from All Saints. In fact, he's had a wilder life than Ricky's in more ways than one.

Another child actor from Anna Scher Theatre, Sid was just a teenager when he got the role in *EastEnders* in 1988. A bit of a party animal in his youth, it was reported in 1996 that his job was on the line after he admitted a £200-a-day cocaine habit.

'I don't just feel lucky to have kept my job,' he said, 'I feel lucky to be alive.'

Now his wild clubbing days are in the past. 'My idea of a good time now is to pull out a bottle of wine and watch a video on my 43-inch TV screen.'

'Just keep smiling'

'Sid do you think they know who we are?'

Sid shares Ricky's passion for motors, but didn't have much luck with them for a time either. First, a 63-year-old pedestrian fell into the path of his BMW, then, in 1998, Sid knocked down an 83-year-old woman when she walked in front of his Vespa scooter. She was knocked unconscious, and Sid visited her in hospital. Thankfully, both pensioners recovered.

In the soap, Ricky's biggest problem had been his family. But when your dad's Frank Butcher and you're married to Bianca, it's no wonder the poor lad has a constant worried frown on his face.

Lurching from one crisis to another, Ricky always tries to do the right thing, and it gets on Sid's wick when people call him thick. After more than ten years he's got earache from hearing it.

'That one's been done to death, ' he moans. 'Ricky Ain't Thicky! Ricky is just a sort of lovable innocent,

Gossip

SID OWEN
(AKA RICKY BUTCHER)

RICKY could briefly be seen puffing on a fag in the show. But his cigarette addiction was seen as a bad example to kids and didn't last.

SID's a bit accident-prone and once nearly sliced off four fingers in a horrifying kitchen knife accident.

AT 14, Ricky appeared in the movie *Revolution* and hung out with its star Al Pacino in New York.

HIS real name is David Owen.

SID's cousin Brian Hagland was brutally murdered on Australia's Bondi Beach.

RICKY had an Indian girlfriend Shireen. In 1989 her father forced them to break up.

really. He's just bungling his way through life the best he can. All right, so he'll never win any prizes for his brain power. So what? He's a good bloke, a good mate to his friends and he can work miracles with motors.'

Playing the role has certainly been good to Sid. An old mate of Patsy Palmer's from their Anna Scher Theatre days, he now lives in a five-bedroom, 16th-century house in Northamptonshire, with its own coach house and barn. 'It's very nice, if I do say so myself,' he smirks.

But that doesn't mean he's in *EastEnders* for life. 'All of us have this need to go off and do other things.'

Still, he'll be enjoying the freedom now his screen missus has gone. 'I know Ricky loves Bianca, but she can be such a domineering cow. He should be allowed to run wild for a while. Maybe become a male escort.'

Dream on, Sid...

Diary
Matthew Norman

I**N what leading new Labour scholars will see**ms the next step in the drive away from trivia, the party is lining up another former soap star for a place on the National Executive. If selected, reports the Sunday Express, Michelle Collins (Cindy Beale in EastEnders, as was) will replace her one-time Albert Square neighbour, Michael Cashman. Michael, a loyalist of unswerving sycophancy (he is widely thought to have a holiday home in Mr Tony's colon) is off to be an MEP. Although Miss Collins is a good egg herself, there are those — sneerers, we call them — who will view her candidacy as High Command cynically using her celebrity to defeat those nasty, grassroots lefties. This is arrant nonsense. In fact, there is a longstanding tradition of Labour relying on actors from soap opera. Minnie Caldwell served at the DEA under George Brown in Harold Wilson's second administration, while Jim Callaghan's first action on becoming prime minister was to bring Albert Tatlock into his Cabinet, as a replacement for the sacked Barbara Castle.

Wot! Soap gets serious?

The Di Marco boys haven't quite got the hang of Walford's traditional dance - the Okey Cokey

In, out, in, out

...shake it all about

Surely no jury would convict her for trying to kill Ian

Michelle Collins (aka Cindy Beale)

Not your typical one-man woman, Cindy wreaked havoc on the male inhabitants of the Square. Raking her fingers through her peroxide hair, you could tell how rough her life was by how badly her roots needed doing. She was the best bitch on the box in a decade packed with scheming, adultery and attempted murder. Well, when you're married to Ian Beale, a girl's gotta have some hobbies.

As feisty off-screen as she is on, though thankfully without the homicidal tendencies, there's never a dull moment around Michelle Collins.

Another star whose eventful private life is played out on the front pages of the tabloids, the nation thrilled to her real-life on/off romance with Fabrizio Tassallini, while watching her brilliantly play the scheming slag of Albert Square.

When Cindy was in town, you could cut the sexual tension with a knife. Whether it was marrying Ian while pregnant with another man's child (oops), taking off to Devon with Wicksy when it dawned on her she'd made a terrible mistake (we could've all told her that), or returning to have twins with Ian, then doing a runner to France with her kids, Cindy was a gal on the pull and on the move.

This, after all, is the woman with a libido so strong that, barely months after giving birth to twins – a feat that would send even the strongest earth mother tottering off to bed for a few early nights – Cindy was stripped down to her cossie and batting her waterproof mascara'd eyelashes at Matt, a swimming pool attendant barely out of

No wonder Cindy lost her kids - dressing them up like this

his teens. Her lipstick was always immaculate too, though God knows how, given the number of furtive snogs she indulged in.

No man stood a chance. But it was in David Wicks that Cindy found a man whose sex drive matched her own, and their rampant romps left the Portacabin groaning.

For actress Michelle, the role was a gift. 'I would rather play strong emotional women than fluffy blonde bimbos. Anyway, I've not got the boobs and I'm not pretty enough to play the bimbos.'

Michelle's path into showbiz started at 16,

when her best friend Kate died of a heart attack. 'It changed me a lot. It made me realise how short life is and how important it is to do what I wanted to do,' she says.

Her dad walked out on her mum when Michelle was a baby, and she's not seen him since, but says you don't miss something you've never had. 'I don't think I suffered in any way. If anything, it made me strong and independent.'

Even so, in her late teens and 20s Michelle suffered from anorexia and depression.

Her turning point was when the producers of a commercial said

Final fade out for Arthur of EastEnders

Gossip

MICHELLE COLLINS
(AKA CINDY BEALE)

CINDY was planned to be in the soap for just 11 weeks.

PRINCESS Diana discussed Cindy's love life on the notorious Squidgygate tapes.

MICHELLE was asked to play Diana in the musical after her death, but said no. 'I was so depressed the day she died I went to see *The Full Monty* to cheer myself up.'

IN 1991 she had a break from *EastEnders* and co-hosted chaotic yoof programme *The Word*.

that she looked like a heroin addict. Shocked, Cindy started working out and getting fit. 'And thankfully I got over it.'

Her big break was

EastEnders in 1988, and she soon learned the hard way about life in the spotlight when ex-lover Nick Fordyce kissed and told to the press. But it was her tempestuous love affair with Fabrizio that was big news.

They met in a Miami disco, and Michelle was soon pregnant. He left his job as a Harley-Davidson salesman and moved to London, but things were difficult.

'We do have a traumatic relationship,' admitted Michelle. 'I'm not the easiest person to live with and nor is Fabrizio. The fact that he is Italian doesn't help.'

Even after their daughter Maia was born in 1996, there were rows. 'Two people who love each other can still destroy each other,' she said. 'It's better to be apart than to bring a child up in an atmosphere where there's arguments all the time.

'I've worked very hard for what I've got and I'm not going to stop. I'd rather bring up

Maia on my own than be trapped in a loveless marriage.'

The couple finally split for good when Maia was two and Michelle says motherhood has mellowed her.

'Having Maia has made me feel so much more secure and has opened me up as a person,' she says. Until you have a child there is definitely something missing in your life. Having a baby has changed me. I'm a bit calmer and less manic and hopefully a nicer person.

'I tend to stay at home more, too. Now I don't want to go out on the town to showbiz parties, but I still like to go out and get a bit wild. Everyone does.'

Especially her *alter ego* Cindy. Michelle reckons Walford's scheming temptress struck a chord because she wasn't Miss Perfect. 'Men liked her because she was dangerous, women liked her because she walked all over men.'

Yet when she left the soap, it was not with a bang, but a whimper. She died off-camera in childbirth, cheating viewers out of what would've been a fantastic deathbed scene.

Michelle had a bit of a tantrum when the news broke that her character was to die, saying that it was outrageous, especially as she was still considering coming back to the show.

But Cindy is no more and Michelle, who lives in Finchley, North London, has moved on with high-profile roles in *Real Women*, *Daylight Robbery*, *Sunburn* and a new sitcom, *Uprising*.

She says her love life is nowhere near as tempestuous as it once was either. 'I'm probably too difficult to handle. I won't cook and I don't wear sexy underwear to bed. I've not got much going for me really...'

Facts

Robbie Williams

In 1995 Robbie Williams appeared briefly at the Queen Vic. Eagle-eyed viewers saw him making a phone call on the pub phone, then chatting at the bar with a mate.

The 'Naked Truth'

The ultimate *EastEnders* 'two-hander', *The Mitchells: Naked Truth* finds Grant and Phil in the Queen Vic after closing, having a brotherly chat. The hour-long video climaxes with Grant and Phil doing a *Full Monty*-style strip to the 1970s disco tune 'Kung Fu Fighting'. You get to see their bums, plus lots of flashbacks and bruvverly bonding.

The Di Marcos

Pasta la vista, baby! The EastEnders girls couldn't believe their luck when Italian stallions Beppe and Gianni di Marco swaggered on to the scene to grab a pizza the action.

Tall, dark and broodingly handsome, they're not averse to giving the Mitchells a run for their money, as well as breaking a few hearts along the way.

The death of their dear old dad meant they had to swap the bright lights of Soho for the slightly dimmer glow of Walford, but before you could say 'You wanna Parmesan cheese with that?' they'd opened an Italian restaurant – despite the fact that most Albert Square residents haven't quite mastered the art of using a knife and fork yet.

The Italian jobbers

'Linsey Dawn McKenzie says yours looks just like this one!'

Michael Greco (aka Beppe Di Marco)

With his strange, precision-shaved goatee, like someone's doodled on his chin, Beppe's job since he was booted out of the police force seems to be rescuing damsels in distress.

First Tiff, then Nina, he's a one-man moral crusade, looking for the kind of fulfilment that a hard day sorting out the scum of Soho as part of the Vice Squad brought him.

In real life, Michael experienced the downside of fame not long after he joined the soap. On

Christmas Day 1998 he left a South London pub and was set upon by three thugs who objected to him flirting with Tiffany.

Shouting, 'We're going to give you some, like Grant gave you,' the men got him in a headlock and took it in turns to punch him. Battered Michael needed an operation to realign his jaw which was fractured in three places.

Onscreen, while Michael may be the new heart-throb on the show, he reckons he's not your regular hunk. 'I'm bow-legged, I don't work out in the gym. I haven't got a six-pack – it's a keg.'

And Michael says his track record with girls was just terrible before *EastEnders*. 'No one fancied me. All the girls thought I was sweet and just wanted to be friends. Now I'm famous there's no shortage of attention. I'm not cynical, but I'm not stupid either.'

He's now acquired the ultimate soap star

Gossip

MICHAEL GRECO
(AKA BEPPE DI MARCO)

Michael helped bring a badly injured girl out of a coma. He visited Tanya Hill five times in hospital, and even arranged for her favourite band East 17 to visit. Tanya's mum believes he helped save her life.

FOR his first scene in the soap, Michael simply had to sip a pint of beer. He was so nervous, he missed his mouth!

HIS best mate is Ian Kelsey, aka Dave Glover in *Emmerdale*. Ian paid off Michael's overdraft when he was a struggling actor, and treated him to a holiday.

HE'S splashed out on a VW Golf with his *EastEnders* earnings.

accessory – a busty Page Three babe in the awe-inspiring 34GG shape of Linsey Dawn McKenzie.

The model has something of a 'colourful' past. She had a torrid affair with Dean (Robbie Jackson) Gaffney, while news of her romps with soccer star Dean Holdsworth didn't do much for his marriage.

But Michael says she's 'loving, warm and sensitive', and after a few teething rucks in public, the couple are now engaged and have just bought a groovy loft-style apartment in North London with a whopping 46ft reception room.

Beppe's love life isn't quite so satisfying. Deserted by Sandra, the mother of his baby son Joe, he picked the wrong bird when he moved in on Tiff. Floored by love rival Grant, he ended up being kicked out of the Vice Squad for destroying vital evidence.

He's yet to learn that being a nice guy gets you nowhere in Walford, but it's only a matter of time before Beppe gets the top babe he so obviously deserves.

I don't know why you're laughing, your freebies are no better!

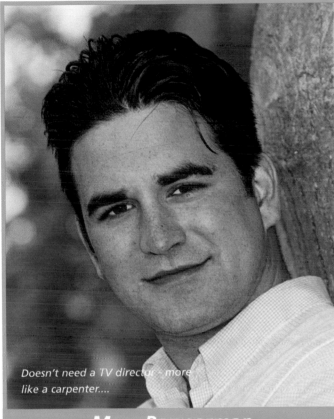

Doesn't need a TV director - more like a carpenter....

Marc Bannerman
(aka Gianni Di Marco)

The Square's resident ladykiller (though not in the Steve Owen sense), this half of the Bolognaise Brothers is a commitment-style macho man whose idea of treating a lady with respect is to wait until she's gone to the loo before he starts to try and pull her mate.
As boss of Italian restaurant Guiseppe's, he's the kind of waiter who uses a giant pepper grinder as a phallic symbol, grinding it suggestively over the meal of any female customer under 50.

Not exactly busy at work, since no one ever eats, watches telly or goes to the loo in soaps, Gianni has plenty of time to chase around the country after his wayward sister Teresa, and pinch the bum of anyone who takes his fancy. Full of cocky charm, he reckons any girl who turns him down is probably a lesbian.

Actor Marc Bannerman is another devoted family man who used his first *EastEnders* pay cheques to help relatives, paying for holidays and helping his sister and brother to buy a flat. In fact, he admits he's as protective of his little sister Karen as Gianni is of Teresa, even though she's 21! 'I'm a great believer in family values.'

Brought up in Finsbury Park, North London, Marc had been out of stage school just 18 months before he got his part as Gianni. He'd been working as a builder until he got his showbiz break.

And privately, his life

seems pretty settled with a long-term offscreen romance with co-star Nadia Sawalha (who plays Annie Palmer). He comforted her after her husband Justin killed himself on Boxing Day 1997, a month after their five-year marriage broke up.

If ever there was a wolf in sheep's clothing...

Leila Birch
(aka Teresa Di Marco)

Who'd be a teenage girl in an Italian family? Poor Teresa spends much of her life being pursued by moral guardians Beppe and Gianni, but then again her taste in men leaves something to be desired.

An old pal of Martine McCutcheon's from Italia Conti drama school, Leila says that it was always her ambition to get on the show and be famous. With an Italian gran, her sultry beauty made her perfect for the part, but so far her onscreen love life has been a disaster.

First there was Tony 'Am I gay or straight?' Hills, but their romantic boating trip down the Norfolk Broads was rather spoilt when his ex-lover Simon came too. Then she and Matthew went on the run with her brother Gianni and Steve Owen in hot pursuit.

Doomed to spend her nights working as a waitress in the Night Café or Guiseppe's, Teresa's love life is going to be a bit limited if every time she meets someone she gets pursued by her overly protective Italian brothers.

For a girl who just wants to have fun, there's been precious little of that so far...

Gossip

LEILA BIRCH
(AKA TERESA DI MARCO)

WHEN she was a teenager, Leila posed as Eve for an art exam wearing just stockings, suspenders, knickers and a couple of fig leaves over her boobs. She was undoubtedly thrilled when a photo found its way into the newspapers.

SHE and her family once booked a holiday to Tenerife and ended up in Marbella.

THE actress is rumoured to be dating *Grange Hill* star Paul Adams.

Carly Hillman
(aka Nicoletta Di Marco)

She's a footie-playing temptress-in-waiting, but though mega-cutie Jamie Mitchell fancied her, Nicky knew her friend Sonia had the hots for him and, in an unlikely show of teenage solidarity, let the chance of a lifetime go. Oddly, she seems to prefer Martin Fowler – though he doesn't return the compliment.

Desperately hoping that trade at Giuseppe's will pick up enough for her to afford a full bottle of Grecian 2000

Louise Jameson
(aka Rosa Di Marco)

It's hard to believe that this harassed mama of the di Marco clan used to be Dr Who's sexy sidekick – actress Louise was once best known for going time travelling in the Tardis.

Now, as the *EastEnders* Italian matriarch, Rosa has a lot on her plate – and it isn't just spaghetti. With no customers in the restaurant, and her bambinos to worry about, she feels very alone since the death of her handsome, charming husband Guiseppe.

Now the poor woman's going white-haired with worry – even donning a scarf and going to mass when she's feeling really down. Her hot-blooded Latin temperament means her idea of a family chat involves hysterical screaming and crashing plates, but now the blood test has proved George Palmer isn't Gianni's dad, she's got one less thing to worry about.

In real life, Louise's seven-year marriage to artist Martin Bedford recently broke up and, with two sons to bring up, she now says she identified with her single-parent screen character.

Even more rats in the kitchen

Grant of EastEnders has tests for malaria

By NEIL SAWYER

EASTENDERS actor Ross Kemp was admitted to hopsital last night after returning from an African holiday with suspected malaria.

The 34-year-old star, who plays hardman Grant Mitchell in the top-rating BBC-1 soap, was under the weather earlier this week when he travelled to Glasgow to campaign for election as rector of its university.

He denied rumours of malaria at the time, saying: 'I have a cold'. But fears about his health have escalated since he returned from a holiday in Tanzania in February.

A spokesman at the Princess Grace Hospital in London, where Kemp was having tests last night said doctors had been unable to establish if he had contracted the disease. 'Mr Kemp is being kept here overnight for observation and the tests have so far proved inconclusive,' she said. 'All being well, he will be allowed to return home tomorrow if it is considered that he does not need further treatment.'

His sudden admission to hospital has meant the actor was forced to pull out of a personal appearance at a nightclub in Swindon, Wiltshire, scheduled for tonight. His agent reportedly told the Kaos club that possible malaria was the cause.

The nightspot's manager Zoltan Branch said: 'Ross was supposed to be coming to Kaos, but his agent rung to say he was calling off because he has malaria.

A spokesman at Kemp's publicists Peters, Fraser and Dunlop said: 'He is having tests. I don't know what the tests are for.'

The malaria scare is not the first bout of ill-health to hit the actor since he shot to fame in EastEnders.

Three years ago he was seen on the Albert Square set hobbling about on crutches after jarring his spine while horse riding.

True to his hardman image, he struggled into work at the Elstree Studios in Hertfordshire despite being in agony.

He was later reported to have consulted a top Harley Street doctor about the painful condition.

Malaria is a disease of the blood caused by a parasite that is transmitted from person to person by the bite of an infected mosquito.

The disease kills millions each year in developing countries and can also cause long-term incapacity. However, cases can also be mild.

Travellers to malaria-affected areas are advised to take tablets which can prevent infection, although even if properly taken they are not always effective because resistance to the drugs has been developed.

Symptoms of malaria include fever, chills, headache, muscle ache, and malaise. Early stages of the disease may resemble the onset of the flu – so travellers returning from infected areas are always advised to treat any aches and pains with caution.

Symptoms can develop as early as six to eight days after being bitten by an infected mosquito, or as late as several months after departure from a malarious area, or after antimalarial drugs are discontinued.

The disease can be treated effectively in its early stages, but delaying treatment can have serious consequences.

Ross Kemp: Taken to hospital

From one insect to another...

"I bet I get drunk and end up with the ugly one..."

She wanted more

CONTINUED FROM PAGE 39

*The trials and
tribulations of
life in the public
eye*

I wanted to marry Scott though he
is 25 years younger. Why did he go?

BARBARA WINDSOR ON HER GREAT LOVE AFFAIRS AND THE RECENT BREAK-UP THAT DEVASTATED HER LIFE

Nice of Rickee to make his mum in law a pair of earings from old car parts down the arches.

Lindsey Jackson (aka Carol Jackson)

A woman who wears a necklace with her name on it in case the fella she's shacked up with that week forgets it, Carol is the slapper of the Square. She never had trouble getting a man, it's keeping 'em that's the problem.

Since the Jackson Five arrived in Walford in 1994, she's spent half her life trying to control her motley brood, and the other half sorting out her bedroom arrangements.

The Tory party's worst nightmare, Carol was a teen mum to Bianca by David Wicks, and got a bit carried away again when the dark-haired Lothario reappeared on the scene. Then she fell for 'Desperate' Dan's beefy charms, blissfully unaware that her hunk had slept with her 15-year-old daughter.

So determined to be with a man, she said yes to his proposal before remembering she was already married; Carol had about five minutes of happiness before it all started to go horribly wrong.

In real life, Lindsey was a hairdresser who dreamed of becoming an actress. She has one young daughter Molly, and had a messy break up with her showbiz agent husband Philip Chard.

She's been romantically linked with ex-*EastEnders* star Michael French (David Wicks) and is now reported to be seeing Patsy Palmer's brother Harry Harris. (What is it with that family and alliteration?)

Lindsey is a lot more glam than the harassed single mum you see on telly, and reckons she's aged years to play her. She's brighter too, saying she quit the show for a while to be with her daughter, and to reclaim her life. 'I never even had time to read a newspaper,

which is very important to me because I am a political animal.' Blimey.

The actress starred in the medical drama *Out of Hours*, but after it flopped she returned to the Square, though she does get fed up with being recognised, 'You can talk to 70 people in one day,' she groans.

If there's one thing Carol's not short of it's stuff to talk about. Leaving Walford as part of the Witness Protection Programme, Carol's marriage to Alan fell apart and now he's fighting for custody of their son Billy.

She's sorted out her appearance a bit – had some highlights, found time to put on a bit of slap – and with Sonia and Robbie still requiring her unique brand of parenting skills ('Your dinner's on the table, I'm off for a shag'), she does her best.

Juggling her career cooking fry-ups in the café with her complicated family life, Carol is '90s woman at her most harassed.

Dan - nice of him to keep Bianca warm for Rickee

Craig Fairbrass (aka Dan Sullivan)

Dan's a man with a dodgy past and a mystery present. Just what does this 'businessman' do all day, and where does he get his money from?

Twice Carol's size, it's also never clear what he sees in the harassed mum-of-four but, as part of one of the most unlikely soap scenarios, he's earned his place in telly history for silencing Bianca's moaning with a passionate snog, and being unable to resist her pallid charms.

For ex-London's Burning star Craig Fairbrass, EastEnders was a chance to get his rugged face back onscreen after a stint in America. Dreaming of being the English Arnold Schwarzenegger, he moved with his family, ex-Page Three wife Elke, and sons Jack and Luke to give Hollywood a shot, but came back home after a series of low budget action movies.

He wasn't too impressed with the LA experience, especially after they stayed in a dodgy part of town. 'All the kids walked around with Uzis. You didn't get a dawn chorus, you got machine-gun fire. I'd grown up in some pretty rough areas but I was petrified.'

The family moved to a nicer area, but though they had Tom and Nicole as neighbours, they were spending so much money on rent they couldn't afford to eat! On the plane home, Craig had just £3 in his pocket...

Another real-life East Ender, Craig's dad was a docker and his mum a machinist, and he had his fair share of trouble as a schoolboy. Expelled, then moved from school to school, he was running wild.

'I just couldn't settle, and teachers told me I'd end up as nothing. I could easily have turned to crime if I hadn't found acting,' he admits. 'Two of my dad's seven brothers knew the Krays. But my uncles all warned me not to mix in those circles.'

Now happily settled in Kent, Craig enjoyed being a bit vulnerable as Dan. 'I fell into the tough guy thing. People forget that I can talk, think and show emotion,' he says (taking out an onion).

Natalie Cassidy
(aka Sonia Jackson)

Growing up in public is never easy (think Corrie's original Martin Platt), and though right now Sonia is not destined for babe status, that never hurt Michelle's chances of getting a snog-fest storyline or two, did it?

At the mo, though, Sonia has little to do but blow her trombone, annoy her brother and sister, pine for Jamie and wind up her mum. She'll have her work cut out in the future though – she's little Liam's godmother!

With a face like that Dean should be in radio

No, sleeping with your husband will not make me feel better...

Dean Gaffney (aka Robbie Jackson)

For a gormless, spotty-faced loser, Robbie hasn't done so bad. He's never going to be a pin-up, but he still managed to have a night of passion in a Southend amusement arcade with a pierced and painted teen temptress, and was bizarrely chosen by Sarah as The One to lose her virginity to. Robbie's now working at the café and living back home with his mum after a brief flirtation with independence when he moved into the squat with Huw and Lenny. (One can only imagine the smell.)

Dean Gaffney's story is rather more, shall we say, colourful. A reformed love rat, the 5ft 5in lad from Richmond, West London, started acting at 13,

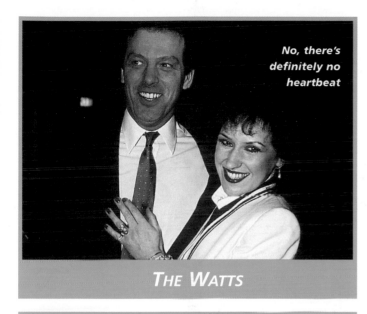

Before her role as Natalie, Lucy had a declining career as a pole dancer

Lucy Speed *(aka Natalie Price)*

Bullied at school by Bianca, short but not sweet, Nat got her own back by sleeping with Ricky. ('She wasn't really a love interest,' says actor Sid Owen chivalrously. 'He just shagged her.') But her karma has hit her in the face and now she 's set up home with Barry, really no life for a young girl. With the dating agency she has a host of other local losers on file, so not much hope for the future, then.

Gossip

LUCY SPEED
(AKA NATALIE PRICE)

NATALIE was once meant to commit suicide on Christmas Day, but the storyline was discarded in case it led to copycat suicides

Theme Park

A theme park in Albert Square? In 1993 it was reported that plans were under way for an American-style extravaganza on the set site in Borehamwood. 'It may not be everyone's idea of the perfect holiday destination, but for *EastEnders* fans it will knock spots off the Bahamas or Bali!' trumpeted the newspapers, unconvincingly.

IT'S A FACT!

IF YOU WANT YOUR SPROG ON TELLY, GIVE BIRTH IN A HOSPITAL NEAR THE *EASTENDERS* STUDIOS IN BOREHAMWOOD, HERTS. WHEN ONE OF THE CAST NEEDS A BABY, THEY CHECK OUT LOCAL NEWBORNS

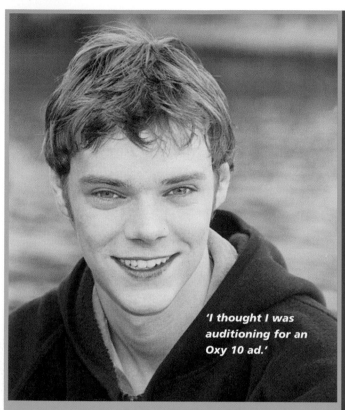

'I thought I was auditioning for an Oxy 10 ad.'

Joe Absolom (aka Matthew Rose)

Oddly, his dad Michael didn't seem to notice. 'You look well,' he said at visiting time.

Joe loves playing the troubled teen, saying, 'I've got one of the meatiest parts in the show. Matthew is falling apart, but for me life couldn't be better.'

Still, he had his doubts about joining EastEnders. 'I had to think long and hard about it. Once you take on something like this, it really does change your life.'

Now he wears a baseball cap over his face when travelling on public transport to avoid being recognised, and says cagily, 'My love life is private, but I do have one.'

His brief stint as a CD-selling entrepreneur and a broken engagement to Sarah Hills behind him, Matthew's young life has gone horribly wrong. He must rue the day he got involved with Steve Owen as DJ at Club E20.

Even before he was witness to the murder and on the run for weeks with Teresa, he was never one to pay much attention to grooming and personal hygiene. But, after a few weeks in prison, he was looking like your classic heroin addict – thin, twitchy and with lank, greasy hair.

Baby Spice

EMMA 'BABY SPICE' BUNTON ONCE APPEARED ON THE SHOW AS A TEENAGE MUGGER.

Her and Ian? The writers are really pushing the limits of credibility this time.

Tamzin Outhwaite
(aka Melanie Healy)

For such a goddess, Mel has somehow ended up with the dregs of Albert Square. She's found herself surrounded by a sea of plastic tat as manager of Beale's Market and, what's worse, not only lives under the same roof as Ian, but actually seems to be dating him.

The long lost sister of Alex the Trendy Vicar, Mel arrived in the Square after six years in the Greek Islands and Ibiza to be reunited with her brother and father Jeff.

Obvious really, after all that sun and Balearic Beat, where else would a babe like Mel end up but swinging Walford?

For Tamzin, 28, the character is fun to play, 'She's out to have a good time and I don't have a problem with that.' Er, going out with Ian is fun?

A real life East Ender, her mum is a financial adviser, and her *EastEnders* break came after eight years as a singer and dancer in West End musicals, including *Oliver* and *Grease*. She has a 'special someone', a director called Marty, 'but it's too early to talk about him.'

EVIL INFLUENCE?

In 1989, a teachers' leader condemned the soap as an evil influence. 'The whole nation is totally drugged by *EastEnders*,' raged Peter Dawson, from the Professional Association of Teachers. 'The programme projects highly deviant forms of behaviour as normal.' And your point is, Peter?

Charlie Brookes
(aka Janine Butcher)

Frank Butcher's daughter, Janine, returned to the Square aged 15, and the greasy Northern diet and rainy climate of Manchester seem to have transformed her from a sulky, silent, skinny, dark and swarthy kid to a fat, pasty, mouthy troublemaker. Her main role in life seems to be winding up Bianca.

Jimi Mistry
(aka Dr Frederico Fonseca)

He may look like he should be in a Liverpool guitar band, but if you fancy the idea of a doctor called Fred with a moptop hairdo who's usually to be found in the Queen Vic propping up the bar, then he's your man with the illegible prescription. He's certainly a lot higher-profile than his predecessor, Dr Legg, who hadn't been seen for years. But is it likely that such a hip hunk wouldn't have noticed Dot was stoned?

Lucy Benjamin
(aka Lisa Shaw)

Bridge Street market inspector Lisa had a fling with Michael Rose, and was gutted when he chose his sick wife over her.

Lucy lives in North London with her boyfriend Jonathan, trained as a dancer and once spent nine months out of work. 'It's character building and a great leveller,' she chirps.

Fears over 'romping Messiah'

NOTED theologians have been privately shown scripts and rough-cut episodes of a powerful three-part drama about the staging of The Passion Plays.

BBC executives were concerned about whether or not some scenes might offend in The Passion, which features rising star Paul Nicholls as an actor hired to portray Jesus in a village drama about the suffering and death of Christ.

What has the Beeb in a state of panic — unnecessarily so in my view — are scenes linking the actor playing Jesus with adultery. The Passion is unofficially scheduled to be screened on BBC1 at Easter but, at present, not Easter Sunday.

Nicholls's character Daniel falls in love with the local dressmaker, played with heartfelt intensity by Gina McKee. She is married with two children and news of the affair splits the close-knit community. But her husband, portrayed by Alastair Galbraith, is all for redemption.

Only those with the iciest eyes will fail to be moved because The Passion is about the power of love and forgiveness.

Miriam Segal, producer of The Passion with film-makers First Choice, told me: 'It's about the Passion Plays rather than religion. It's based on the original texts and we take them very seriously.'

The cast is superb, from Freddie Jones, as the farmer who plays God, to Jemima Rooper as Gina's daughter.

I think it's a breakthrough for Nicholls, who used to play Joe Wicks in EastEnders. Audiences are going to enjoy watching him, especially when in romp mode or skinny-dipping in a lake.

Mr Nicholls will have two films, Somme and The Clandestine Marriage, at the Cannes Film Festival in May.

Object of desire: Star Paul Nicholls

■ THE corn is as gloriously high as an elephant's eye again with Oklahoma! at the Lyceum on the Strand after its triumphant run at the National Theatre last year.

Hugh Jackman is back as Curly and so is Josefina Gabrielle as his Laurey. Maureen Lipman, Jimmy Johnston and Shuler Hensley are also returning. Cameron Mackintosh has dedicated the production to Jamie Hammerstein — whose father Oscar wrote the lyrics — who died recently. After the six-month run in London, the hope is that American Equity will allow the entire cast to bring Oklahoma! to Broadway as a special ensemble, to be replaced by American actors after three months.

Then late in the year, Sky Films will premiere a TV version of the National show, which will be released on video later.

OK let's get serious....

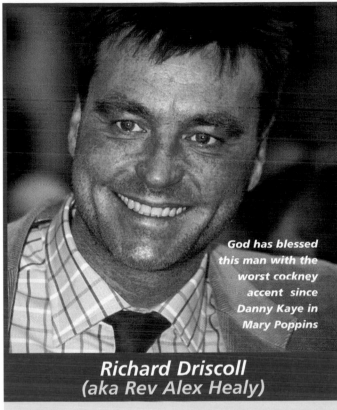

God has blessed this man with the worst cockney accent since Danny Kaye in Mary Poppins

Richard Driscoll
(aka Rev Alex Healy)

Cockney vicar who's main claim to fame is sleeping with Kathy and having a megababe for a sister. Off to Somalia to save souls.

Troy Titus-Adams
(aka Nina Harris)

Irene's ex-prostitute niece, a nice girl who's doing A-levels in the hope of becoming a probation officer. Brings out the best in Grant and does a good line in thin-lipped angst as her past comes back to haunt her in the dubious shape of dodgy Dean.

BEER BAN

The Queen Vic stopped serving real booze in 1994, replacing draught beer with a non-alcoholic lookalike called pub shandy. An 'insider' said: 'It won't be much fun without booze to help things along (hic).'

IT'S A FACT!

THE STORYLINES ARE PLANNED SIX MONTHS IN ADVANCE AND FILMING STARTS SIX WEEKS BEFORE IT APPEARS ON TELLY.

BADDIES

Who'd be an East End villain? Actor John Altman copped constant abuse from people confusing him with his racist, murdering, junkie scumbag character Nick Cotton, while William Boyd, who played upper-class rapist James Wilmott Brown reckoned his TV career was wrecked because viewers so hated him.

Then the wind changed

'I've stopped smoking!'

June Brown
(aka Dot Cotton)

The Square's resident busybody, Dot's been let down badly by her nearest and dearest. Husband Charlie was a waste of space, and son Nick turned out to be such a wrong 'un, that when she won £10,000 at bingo, he tried to poison her.

Now, suffering from glaucoma and running around in her dark glasses like some demented rock chick, she's the only character on telly you can rely on to be puffing away on a regular basis. (Just don't mention her taste for waccy baccy!)

Actress June is a shameless smoker offscreen too. A 60-a-day addict she smoked through both her pregnancies, had a fag in the delivery room after giving birth, and even lights up in bed.

Gossip

JUNE BROWN
(AKA DOT COTTON)

JUNE Brown wanted to be an osteopath but couldn't stick the studying, so she joined the Wrens and caught the acting bug in a revue for the sailors.

'For how many minutes?'

Prat in a hat

Peter Dean
(aka Pete Beale)

Too many late nights watching videos, Nigel.

Paul Bradley
(aka Nigel Bates)

He played Pauline's twin and dozy fruit'n'veg seller in the show, but big-mouth actor Pete went from £70,000 a year to £44 week on the dole when he was killed off after blabbing to *The Sun* about the show's behind-the-scenes rows. (He told the newspaper he hated Leslie Grantham so much he'd like to kill him.) His acting career never recovered and in February 1998 he was spotted earning £6 an hour as a car park attendant in Essex.

Paul studied at Manchester University with pals Rik Mayall, Ade Edmondson and Ben Elton. He once played guitar in a band called Sellotape and the Kippers.

10 THINGS THEY'LL NEVER SAY...

1. YOU GOT AN ASHTRAY, STEVE?

2. BEEN ANOTHER QUIET YEAR IN THE SQUARE, AIN'T IT?

3. I'M WORRIED ABOUT DOT – I THINK SHE'S TURNED INTO A GYM JUNKIE

4. PAULINE? SHE'S GONE TO THE PRADA SALE WITH TARA PALMER-TOMPKINSON

5. BUT RICKY, I REALLY MUST CHALLENGE YOU ON THAT POINT. TONY BLAIR'S FISCAL POLICY WITH REGARDS TO THE EURO IS ACTUALLY A BRILLIANT PIECE OF MONETARY BRINKMANSHIP

6. DID YOU SEE CORRIE LAST NIGHT?

7. THAT CAROL JACKSON IS A ONE-MAN WOMAN

8. OI, PHIL, YOU NEED A HAIRCUT

9. ISN'T THAT POSH SPICE AT THE BAR?

10. NAH, DON'T TELL ME, I KNOW EXACTLY WHAT'S GOING ON

IT'S A FACT!
THE LATEST HITS GET PLAYED IN THE PUB AND CAFE BECAUSE THE SHOW GETS ADVANCE COPIES OF RELEASES FROM RECORD COMPANIES

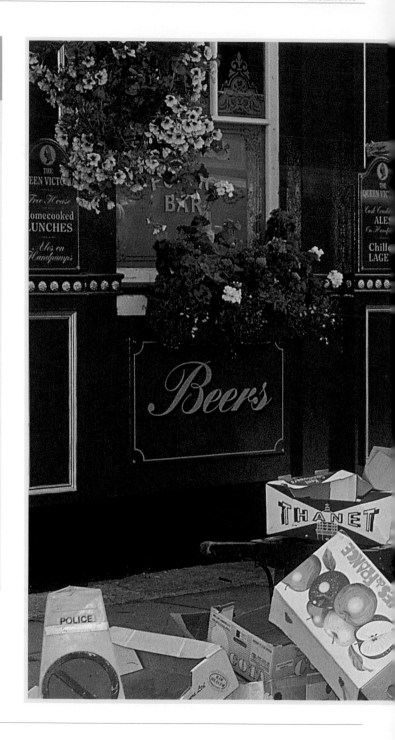

NSAGENTS * GROCERS * OFF LICENCE

Tesco's must be petrified.

I may have HIV - but I'm gonna be around for more episodes than you...

Tony - the best ever advertisement about the dangers of taking drugs

Put it back, now!

IF YOU ENJOYED THIS BOOK, WHAT ABOUT THESE!

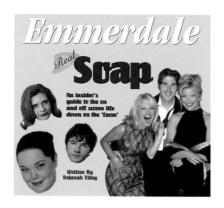

All these books are available at your local bookshop or can be ordered direct from the publisher. Please list the titles you require and give your name and address, including postcode.

Please send to Generation Publications Ltd, 11-12 Tottenham Mews, London W1P 1PJ, a cheque or postal order for £7.99 for each book and add the following for postage and packaging:
UK – £1 for the first book, 50p for the second and 30p for the third and for each additional book.
OVERSEAS – £2 for the first book, £1 for the second and 50p for each additional book.